NATIVE AMERICAN LEATHER & BEAD CRAFTING

NATIVE AMERICAN LEATHER & BEAD CRAFTING

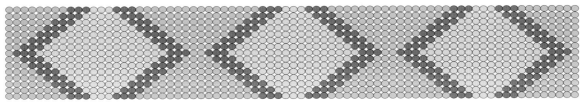

PATTY COX

STERLING

New York / London
www.sterlingpublishing.com

Prolific Impressions Production Staff:
Editor in Chief: Mickey Baskett
Copy Editor: Phyllis Mueller
Graphics: Karen Turpin
Styling: Lenos Key
Photography: Jerry Mucklow
Administration: Jim Baskett

Library of Congress Cataloging-in-Publication Data

Cox, Patty, 1956-
  Native American leather & bead crafting / Patty Cox.
     p. cm.
  Includes index.
  ISBN-13: 978-1-4027-3519-6
  1. Indian craft--United States. 2. Leatherwork. 3. Beadwork. I. Title.

TT23.C6735 2008
745.5--dc22

                                                        2007048198

10 9 8 7 6 5 4 3 2 1

Published by Sterling Publishing Co., Inc.
387 Park Avenue South, New York, NY 10016
©2008 by Prolific Impressions, Inc.
Distributed in Canada by Sterling Publishing
c/o Canadian Manda Group, 165 Dufferin Street
Toronto, Ontario, Canada M6K 3H6
Distributed in the United Kingdom by GMC Distribution Services
Castle Place, 166 High Street, Lewes, East Sussex, England BN7 1XU
Distributed in Australia by Capricorn Link (Australia) Pty. Ltd.
P.O. Box 704, Windsor, NSW 2756, Australia

Printed in China
All rights reserved

Sterling ISBN 978-1-4027-3519-6

For information about custom editions, special sales, premium and corporate purchases, please contact Sterling Special Sales Department at 800-805-5489 or specialsales@sterlingpublishing.com.

Patty Cox

Patty is a multi-talented artist whose orientation is in graphics and illustration but is adept at beading, jewelry making, gardening, and a variety of crafts. Her forte is taking a new product, finding out its capabilities and designing projects or patterns for its use. She has designed several fabric groups for a leading textile manufacturer. Patty is $1/16$th Cherokee and has enjoyed her research for this book and learning about her heritage.

Patty is the creative force behind P.Cox Design Studio. She has authored and illustrated numerous storybooks for children. One of the children's books she authored and illustrated is entitled "Gift of Hope" (©1995), a story about a young Native American girl and a white buffalo calf who set out on a journey to teach people everywhere to be a strong thread in the web of life. The book includes several Native American craft projects that young readers can create.

About the Contributors

◆ Cynthia Lee

Cindy Lee has been trained in a variety of arts and crafts techniques. She now concentrates most of her work in creating fine art on gourds. There is a rich and varied cultural heritage in the use and decoration of gourds that inspires Cindy's work. Several years ago, while teaching weaving for an environmental living program, the discussion moved to baskets, and then to the use of gourds by pioneers and Native Americans. After some research and experimenting she became captivated by the artistic possibilities of hard shell gourds. She teaches gourd art classes at the Caning Shop in Berkeley, CA and Zittel Farms in Folsom.

Before gourds, Cindy was an award winning painter, using soft pastels as her medium. She has also had success designing polymer clay jewelry of people's pets. Occasionally she also gives private drawing lessons.

◆ Martha Berry

Martha Berry is a Cherokee beadwork artist. At the age of five, her mother and grandmother began teaching her to use a needle and thread. By age nine, she was making her own clothes, and at twenty, she was a seamstress for a touring ice show.

Born to Cherokee/English/Scotch-Irish parents and raised in northeastern Oklahoma, Martha took her Cherokee heritage for granted for many years. In her forties, her children nearly grown, she began to discover the richness and importance of her ancestors' experience and turned her skill with a needle to beadwork.

Martha divides her time between research and creating beadwork inspired by the styles of the Southeastern Woodland Native American Indians. Her beadwork often illustrates the stories and lore of her Cherokee ancestors. She has received numerous awards and prizes for her work, which is widely exhibited and collected. A registered tribal citizen of the Cherokee Nation, she lives in Texas with her husband, Dave, a journalist.

Special thanks to **Orrin Lewis** and **Laura Redish** for their diligence in their attempts to keep the native languages alive through their website www.native-languages.org.

CONTENTS

Influenced by Traditional Beauty

Native American art has a timeless appeal and fascinates anyone who appreciates quality crafting and beautiful design. The art is complex, combining crafting skills with traditional designs that are derived from nature and often have spiritual meaning. Many Native Americans still work in traditional ways to make fine, museum-quality works of art. The work of these artists is sanctioned and protected by the U.S. Department of Interior. Their products are available in shops, on their reservations, at museums, and through on-line sources. See "The Indian Arts & Crafts Act of 1990" for more information.

The projects in this book are NOT Indian made or designed, but are, instead, modern crafters' interpretations of traditional Native American designs and techniques. The projects were created with respect and are intended to honor Native American traditions and skills. They use techniques, supplies, and tools that are accessible to any crafter. We have included information gleaned from a variety of sources that is intended to foster an appreciation for the historical significance of Native American arts and crafts. While teaching the crafter modern techniques, we hope also to pass on interesting information about symbols, materials, and processes that were used by particular tribes.

Even though the inspiration for these designs may be centuries old, they look fresh and contemporary – not out of place – in today's fashion world. Because they are made with natural products, the articles of clothing, footwear, belts, jewelry, bags, and vessels are classics that never seem to go out of style. Crafters who wish to learn some of the ancient techniques of working with leather and beads can re-create beautiful adornments.

American Indian Clothing and Regalia*

Originally, there were many different traditional clothing styles in North America. Nearly every Native American tribe had its own distinctive style of dress, and the people could often tell each other's tribal identities by looking at their clothes, headdresses, and ornamentation.

In most tribes, Native American men wore **breechclouts or breechcloths** (a long rectangular piece of hide or cloth tucked over a belt, so that the flaps fell down in front and behind), sometimes with leather **leggings** attached in colder climates. In other tribes Indian men wore a short kilt or fur trousers instead of a breechcloth. Most Indian men did not use shirts, but Plains Indian warriors wore special buckskin **war shirts** decorated with ermine tails, hair, and intricate quillwork and beadwork.

Most Native American women wore **skirts and leggings**, though the length, design, and material of the skirts varied from tribe to tribe. In some Indian cultures women's shirts were option- al and were usu- 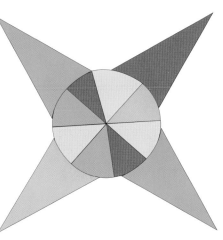 ally treated more like coats, while in others, women always wore tunics or mantles in public. And in other tribes women usually wore **one-piece dresses** instead, like the Cheyenne buckskin dress. Nearly all Native Americans had some form of **moccasin** (a sturdy leather shoe) or **mukluk** (a heavier boot), with the styles of footwear differing from tribe to tribe.

Most tribes used **cloaks** in colder weather, but some of the northern tribes wore Inuit-style **fur parkas** instead. Most variable of all were **headgear** and **formal clothing**, which were different in nearly every tribe.

After colonization, Native American clothes began to change. For one thing, as Indian tribes were driven from their ancient lands and forced into closer contact with each other, they began to borrow some of each other's tribal dress, so that fringed buckskin clothing, feather headdresses, and woven blankets became popular among Indians outside of the tribes in which they originated. For another, Indians began to adapt some articles of Euro- pean costume to their own style, decorating cloth garments with characteristic Native American beadwork, embroidery, and designs. These clothes were not original to the Ameri- cas, but by the 1800s they were recognized by anyone view- ing them as Indian apparel. Such post-colonial native dress includes beaded jackets and shirts, ribbon shirts, Seminole patchwork skirts, satin shawls, woolen sweaters, broad ribbon applique, jingle dresses, and the Cherokee tear dress.

Today, most Native Americans wear contemporary American and Canadian clothes in their daily life; however, unique American Indian clothing styles still exist. Some traditional Indian garments, such as buckskins, ribbon dresses, and beaded moccasins, are still worn in many tribes, particularly to formal events. Others, such as breechcloth,

Continued on next page

The Indian Arts & Crafts Act of 1990

The Indian Arts & Crafts Act of 1990 (Public Law No. 101-644) is a truth-in-advertising law that prohibits misrepresentation in the marketing of Indian arts and crafts products in the United States. It is illegal to offer, display for sale, or sell any art or craft product in a manner that falsely suggests the art or craft product is Indian-produced, an Indian product, or the product of a particular Indian or Indian tribe or Indian arts and crafts organization resi- dent within the United States. For a first-time violation of the Act, an individual can face civil or criminal penalties up to a fine of $250,000 or a five-year prison term or both. If a business violates the Act, it can face civil penalties or can be prosecuted and fined up to $1,000,000.

Under the Act, an Indian is defined as any member of any federally or state recognized Indian Tribe or an individ- ual certified as an Indian artisan by any Indian Tribe. The law covers all Indian and Indian-style traditional and contemporary arts and crafts produced after 1935. The Act broadly applies to the marketing of arts and crafts (including, but not limited to Indian-style jewelry, pottery, baskets, carved stone fetishes, woven rugs, kachina dolls, and clothing) by any person in the United States.

Continued from page 9

leggings, headdress and dance shawl, are only worn at powwows and religious ceremonies. In general, American Indians use the word "regalia" for traditional clothing that is used for ceremonial occasions. Some native people find the phrase "Native American costume" offensive, due to long association with hurtful red-faced Halloween costumes.

Native American Beadwork*

Originally, Native American beads were carved from shells, coral, turquoise and other stones, copper and silver, wood, amber, ivory, and animal bones, horns, and teeth. Glass beads were not used until the colonists brought them from Europe 500 years ago, but like horses, they quickly became part of American Indian culture. Today glass beads, particularly fine seed beads, are the primary materials for traditional beaders of many tribes.

There are as many different Native American beading traditions, designs, styles and stitches as there are tribes and nations. Plains Indian beadwork is best known, with its intricate peyote stitch beading and bone hairpipe chokers, but there are beadwork traditions throughout North America, from the wampum belts of the eastern Indians to the dentalium strands of the west coast Indians, from the floral beadwork of the northern Indians to the shell and turquoise heishi beads of the southwest Indians, and everything in between. Beads were a common trade item since ancient times, so it wasn't surprising to see abalone shells from the west coast in Cherokee beadwork or quahog wampum from the east coast in Ojibway beadwork, even before the Europeans arrived and forced disparate tribes into closer contact with each other.

As a great generalization, native **beadwork** can be grouped into beaded **leather** (usually clothing, moccasins, or containers) and beaded **strands** (usually used for jewelry, but sometimes also as ornamental covering to wrap around a gourd or other ceremonial or art object) For beaded leather arts, Indian craftspeople sew each bead onto a leather backing (or cloth, today).

Contributed by Orrin Lewis and Laura Redish from their website www.native-languages.org.

A related craft, **quillwork**, involved softening and dying stiff porcupine quills and affixing them to leather, to birch bark, or to other crafts. Indian quillwork largely died out as an art form when seed beads became available to the northern and Plains tribes, but today some native artists are taking a renewed interest in quilling.

As for beaded strands, Indian craftspeople stitch the beads together into strings or a mesh, using sinew, thread, or wire. Beading strands and beading onto leather are very complicated, time-consuming and delicate tasks that require many years of practice to do well.

Cherokee Beadwork

In the mid-1600s, the Cherokee began trading with the colonists for European glass seed beads, steel needles, silk thread and ribbon, and cloth made of wool, cotton, and linen. Along with other tribes that lived in the area that would become the southeastern United States, they began to produce unique, exquisite beadwork. The art form evolved and matured by the end of the 1700s, and enjoyed its peak between 1800 and 1840. The exchange of bandolier bags, like the ones shown on these pages, became important on Southeastern Woodlands tribal diplomatic protocol. Known recipients included tribal chiefs, a U.S. Army general, and a U.S. Navy officer.

By 1840, the tribes of the southeast had been forcibly removed from their ancestral homeland, an event called the Indian Removal that became known as the Trail of Tears because the Cherokees called it "the trail where we cried." One in four Cherokees died during this relocation. Following the Removal, the Cherokees abandoned their beautiful beaded art. Faced with rebuilding their homes, farms, and families, there was little time or energy for making beaded moccasins, bandolier bags, sashes, belts, or leggings. The loss of this art form was so complete that, by the end of the 20th century, very few Cherokees were able to recognize their own ancestors' beadwork.

Happily, traditional pre-1840 Southeastern Woodlands beadwork is enjoying a revival among 21st century Cherokee, Creek, and Seminole people, and traditional beaders, collectors, and brokers are active all across the United States. The two bandolier bags on these pages are vibrant examples of that revival.

Ani Yunwiya, a beaded bandolier bag by Martha Berry
Dimensions: Approx. 36" high x 15" wide x 2" deep
Materials: Wool, cotton calico, Czech glass seed beads, cotton binding, yarn, trade beads.
Photo by Dave Berry

The Story of Ani Yunwiya

This bag was inspired by a bandolier bag that now resides in the Colter Bay Indian Museum, Grand Teton National Park. Around the year 1840, a Cherokee beader, probably a woman, created that bandolier bag. She used red wool, calico cloth, glass seed beads, ribbon, and yarn. The design motifs she chose were floral, in pink, green, dark blue, and white beads. Sometime over the years, the bag lost its strap and all but one tassel, and became a part of the David T. Vernon collection.

This new bag, called *Ani Yunwiya* is unique. For the strap, the artist created symbolic floral motifs. Like the Cherokee people, these motifs are plants in full bloom, but with their roots in two different places.

The Story of The Plants Became Allies

by Martha Berry

The Plants Became Allies is a tribute to the generous gift from the plants to the humans based on a traditional Cherokee story, The Origin of Disease. The story recounts a time when humans, animals, and plants lived in balance and harmony with one another. That balance was destroyed when humans invented weapons, began killing more animals than they could eat, and neglected the important tradition of honoring the animals' spirits. To gain revenge on humans, the story goes, animals created disease. The plants, knowing the destruction of the delicate balance meant the destruction of them all, became allies to the humans – each plant volunteered to give itself to cure a disease and to reveal the cures to humans. This act restored the delicate balance, and life went on.

This bandolier bag includes all elements of the life of a plant – seed, vine, bud, blossom and full flower – growing in a counter-clockwise direction around the bag. From the spring green tassels at the bottom, "growing up" to the autumnal gold edging at the top, the cycle of life is also seen. The materials, beading style, and techniques used are authentic to the pre-1840 era.

The Plants Became Allies, a beaded bandolier bag by Martha Berry
Dimensions: Approx. 36" high x 15" wide x 2" deep
Materials: All materials are authentic (pre-1840 era): European glass seed beads, saved-edge stroud wool, silk ribbon, cotton calico, cotton yarn, brass trade beads.
Photo by Dave Berry

BEADWORK TECHNIQUES

Here is a sampling of techniques that are used to create the beautiful beadwork done by Native American artists. Today glass beads, particularly fine seed beads, are the primary materials for traditional beaders of many tribes. There are as many different Native American beading traditions, designs, styles and stitches as there are tribes and nations. Plains Indian beadwork is best known, with its intricate peyote stitch beading and bone hairpipe chokers, but there are many beadwork traditions used throughout North America. Here we have pinpointed some of the most used techniques and supplies for creating projects inspired by Native American designs.

Beading Supplies

Glass Beads

Glass beads were brought to America by European colonists. The most common type of glass beads are seed beads. They are small, short glass beads that are made from tubes, cut, and heated until smooth. They are sized by number; the smaller the number, the larger the bead. Size 11 is a good, all-purpose size. Choose high-quality seed beads for best results. E beads are larger-size seed beads

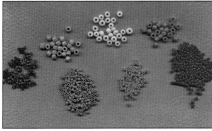

Top row: E beads
Bottom row: Seed beads

Bone Beads

Bones of animals, particularly birds, have long been used to make beads.

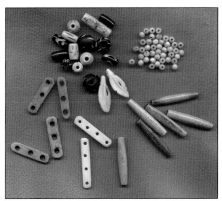

Pictured clockwise from top left: carved beads, 4mm round, hairpipe beads, bone spacers, pictured at center: carved bone feather pendants.

Horn Beads

Horn beads were made from the horns of animals.

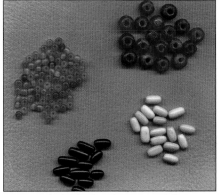

Pictured clockwise from top left: 4mm gold beads, 8mm beads, 4x8mm antiqued rice horn beads, 4x8mm black rice horn beads.

Metal Beads

Metal beads may be made of gold, silver, brass, copper, or mixed metals or may be plated over a base metal. They come in many shapes and finishes.

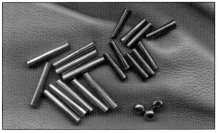

Pictured: Brass and aluminum cones, brass beads

Pictured: Brass and aluminum cones, brass beads, conchos

Turquoise & Coral

Turquoise and coral are natural, semi-precious gemstones. They may appear as large or small nuggets or as polished beads.

Pictured clockwise from top left: turquoise beads, turquoise nuggets, bamboo coral nuggets, coral branch beads

Shell Beads

Beads carved from shells were used as currency (wampum) and for jewelry-making. Wampum beads were made by eastern tribes in two colors, white (from whelk shells) and purple-black (from quahog shells). Abalone shell beads were made by western tribes.

"Heishi" originally meant "Shell," but came to be known as small shells that were ground and shaped into beads and drilled with a hole in the center for stringing. Today "heishi" can refer to beads made of natural materials. It is thought that heishi beads are the oldest form of jewelry in New Mexico, with the origin being the Santo Domingo and San Felipe Pueblo Indians.

Pictured clockwise from top left: 4-5mm mosaic tube beads, clamshell heishi, dark penshell heishi, mother of pearl nuggets, spiral shells, cowrie shells, pictured at center: shell sticks.

Beading Supplies, continued from page 15.

Needles, Thread & Wire

Beading needles are long, thin needles especially made to pass through the holes of beads. They come in different lengths and sizes. The larger the number, the smaller the diameter. A size 10 or 12 beading needle will easily go through size 11 seed beads. **Beading thread** is made of strong twisted nylon. Some thread comes pre-waxed; other threads should be waxed with beeswax or a special thread wax to keep them from tangling. **Beading wire** is manufactured specifically for beading. Strong and hypoallergenic, it is made of woven strands of stainless steel wire and coated in nylon. It comes in different diameters.

Native American Glass Bead Use

The Natives began accepting glass beads from the trading Europeans, placing a high value on these beads. They attributed symbolic meaning to the beads because of the bead properties – such as color, form and the materials used. The beads were incorporated into the exiting cultural and religious ideologies. The beads were viewed as prestige and luxury items and indicated wealth because of the origin or the beads, the distance the bead traveled, and the myths associated with the European ships that brought the beads.

Beading Loom

A beading loom makes it easy to do.

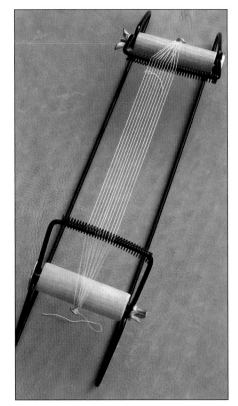

Shown: beading loom with attached warp threads.

Tools

You'll need pliers and wire cutters for making jewelry. Round nose pliers have rounded ends for forming wire loops. Needlenose pliers have flat inner surfaces and pointed ends. Use wire cutters or the cutting edges of pliers for cutting wire.

Peyote Beadwork

Peyote beadwork is a style of beadwork long used to cover and adorn three-dimensional objects like gourds (it is sometimes called "gourd stitch") and the handles of items such as fans, rattles, and sticks used in rituals of the Native American (peyote) church. Most often, the peyote stitch is used to form hollow cylinders for earrings or neck medallions with glass seed beads.

Peyote beadwork starts with a line or circle of beads on a single thread. Additional beads are added in rows, with the beads in each new row stitched so they fall between the beads of the previous row. For an example, see the "Peyote Stitch Arrowhead Amulet."

The diagram here is the single needle, single-thread technique. Bringing the needle back through alternate beads to form the next row creates a diamond pattern. 1) String an even number of beads. 2) Pick up bead and then go through the second bead from the end. Continue on, going through every other bead. This forms 3 rows because of the way the skipped beads drop down to form a row. 3) To make the 4th row, when you get to the end, pick up a bead and then go through the last bead added. Continue adding a bead before going through the new beads added.

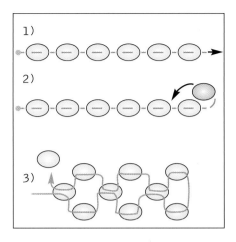

Loom-Woven Beadwork

Loom-woven beadwork is made by warping a tension loom with beading thread and using a threaded needle to string beads across the warp threads on the loom. It's a three-step process; numerous examples appear throughout this book.

Step 1 – Warping the Loom
Warp threads run the length of the loomed beadwork and are on each side of each bead. To determine the number of warp threads, count the number of beads on each line of a beaded design. (The Beading Charts that accompany each project will show you.) Add one more thread to the bead count. (Example: A row of 31 beads will require 32 warp threads.) The warp threads need to be as long as the length of the finished piece of beadwork plus about 6". (Example: A 6½" piece of beaded work requires 12½" warp threads.)

To attach the beading thread, tie the end around the screw on the end of the loom. Bring the warp thread over the spring wire and run it through the spring wire at the other end of the loom. Wrap the thread around the screw at that end of loom. Continue adding threads until you have attached the specified number.

Step 2 – Beading
Thread a beading needle with about 36" beading thread. Tie the end of the thread to the outer warp thread on the loom. Thread first row of beads on the needle according to the Beading Chart for your project. Pass the row of beads on the thread *under* the warp threads and perpendicular to them. Press the beads up between the warp threads with your finger. Thread the needle back through the beads, passing the thread *over* the warp threads. Continue, following the Beading Chart, until you have beaded all the rows.

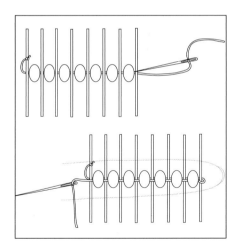

Step 3 – Ending
After the final row is beaded, tie off the beading thread on the outside warp thread. Place cellophane tape around the warp threads above the beginning beads and below the ending beads to securely hold the beads in place. Remove the beaded work from the loom.

Continued on page 18.

Bead Applique

There are many ways of sewing beads onto leather or fabric. A beading needle is used that is threaded with either beading thread or sinew (natural or artificial.) Here are three popular ways of bead appliqué to create designs.

Fret Edging

The fret edge is a beading technique used to decorate edges of leather. Modern beaders sometimes call it the zipper edge because the placement of the beads resembles the teeth of a zipper.

1. Thread a beading needle with beading thread. Knot one end. Bring up the needle from the underside of the edge of the leather or fabric. Thread three beads on the needle. Bring the needle back through the suede edge leaving a space of one bead from the starting thread. Thread the needle back through the last bead. (Fig. 1)
2. Add two beads 1) and bring the needle back down. (Fig. 2)
3. Repeat the process as you work around the edge of piece. When finished, tie off the thread.

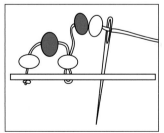
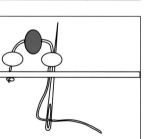

Lane Stitch Applique

This is sometimes called a "lazy" stitch because of its ease of application – multiple beads are sewn onto the fabric at once, rather than sewing on one bead at a time. It is a very common appliqué technique seen in many museum pieces. This stitch has been traced back to the early 1800's when the Native Americans used the seed beads they received from the white traders to make designs on their clothing and other articles.

This is a way of sewing beads onto a surface, following a pattern. Rather than sewing on one bead at a time, five to seven beads are placed on the needle at once. The needle passes through the thickness of the leather to conceal threads.

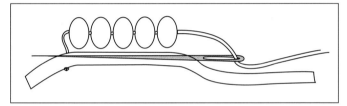

Two-Needle Applique

You can do two-needle applique directly on a leather surface or on heavy-weight interfacing.

1. Thread two beading needles with beading thread.
2. Take up several beads on one thread.
3. Use the second threaded needle to stitch the strand to the surface every two or three beads.

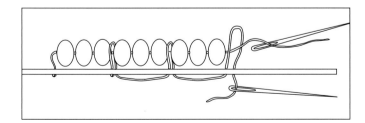

WORKING WITH LEATHER

Native Americans used leather for so much of their housing, clothing, ceremonial items, bags, pouches, shoes. It was sturdy, easy to come by, and could be decorated beautifully with beading. Today, leather is still a prized fabric. Leather and leather crafting supplies are readily available online or in specialty crafting shops.

With mobile tribes, such as the Plains Indians, possessions had to be carried and moved from camp to camp. Leather was an excellent fabric to make bags for carrying these possessions. The bags were various sizes for specific purposes. The women decorated these bags with care and meaning using symbols or designs to identify a particular tribe.

Leather Crafting Supplies

Leather

The animal skins used for crafting are made of tanned leather from the skins of cows, sheep, deer, goats, elk, or goats that have been exposed to a natural vegetable or chemical bath. Tanning gives leather flexibility, strength, durability, and stretchability. Leather has many grades, colors, textures, and weights. You can purchase leather as complete hides, small skins, or small crafting pieces. Pre-cut, narrow strips of leather are called lacing.

Cutting Tools

- **Scissors** can cut thin suedes and garment leather.

- **Leather shears** are useful for cutting heavier leathers.

- A **rotary cutter** can be used to make straight cuts and fringe on thinner leathers; thicker leathers should be cut with a **craft knife**.

- A **straight edge**, such as a metal ruler with a cork back, is useful for guiding the blade of a rotary cutter or craft knife.

- Cutting mat – A self-healing mat with grid markings makes cutting easier when you use a rotary cutter or craft knife.

Leather Crafting Supplies

Needles & Sinew

Needles for hand sewing leather are called leather needles or glover's needles. They have a triangular, sharp end that eliminates the need for prepunching leather.

Sinew is used for hand sewing. Natural sinew, from the ligaments and tendons of deer and elk, is rarely used today because the process for making it is tedious and time-consuming. Today, crafters use artificial sinew. Made of synthetic material, it is strong, comes in a variety of colors, and is easy to use. It can be split into finer strands, if desired.

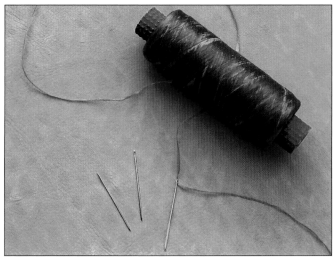

Pictured: Glover's needles and sinew.

Leather Punches

Leather punches are used for making holes in leather. There are rotary punches available that will make holes in a variety of diameters. You can also find single hole-size punches. It is much easier if you punch holes in the leather when you are sewing or lacing pieces together. You will also need to punch holes in the leather when attaching snaps or fasteners.

Cutting Leather

Thinner leathers can be easily cut with scissors, leather shears, or a rotary cutter.

Cutting leather on a cutting mat, using a rotary cutter.

Using a rotary tool and straight edge to cut fringe.

LEATHER & BEAD PROJECTS

Here are 36 projects that have been inspired by Native American tribes, designs, and the materials they used. The projects in this book are NOT Indian made or designed; but are meant to honor their traditions and skills. Traditional techniques have been updated for today's materials. It is our intention to help foster an appreciation for the historical significance of the Native American arts and crafts. While teaching the crafter modern beading techniques, we hope also to pass on some interesting information about tradition and techniques — why certain symbols or materials were used by particular tribes, while other materials and techniques were embraced in other tribes. We hope you enjoy the making and using of the projects created in this book.

Pictured opposite:
Great Lakes Pouch.
See page 32 for
instructions.

CHUMASH-INSPIRED SHELL NECKLACE

The Chumash Indians lived on the coastal areas and islands of southern California near what is now Santa Barbara. They were hunter-gatherers who specialized in fishing and built seaworthy plank canoes. Malibu and Simi Valley are place names with origins from Chumash words. Remains of the Chumash culture, including rock paintings, can be seen, and their baskets are prized by collectors and exhibited in museums.

This shell necklace recalls the tribe's life near the sea. The finished length is 26".

SUPPLIES

◆ 58 shell sticks, 15mm to 35mm
◆ 99 puka shells, 8mm *or* white heishi shell beads
◆ 38" bead stringing wire
◆ 2 silver crimp beads
◆ 2 silver beads, 3mm
◆ Silver clasp
◆ Needlenose pliers

INSTRUCTIONS

1. Thread a crimp bead on the length of beading wire. Thread one end of the wire through one side of the clasp, then back through the crimp bead, leaving a 1½" tail. Crimp the bead next to the clasp.
2. Thread a 3mm silver bead and 21 puka shells on the wire and over the wire tail.
3. Place alternating shell sticks and puka shells on the wire, graduating the sizes so the smallest shell sticks are on the ends and the largest shell stick is in the center of the necklace.
4. End the necklace with 21 puka shells and a silver bead.
5. Thread a crimp bead on the end of the wire. Thread the wire through the other side of the clasp, then back through the crimp bead, the silver bead, and several shell beads. Pull wires taut. Crimp bead. Cut wire tail. ❑

COMANCHE-INSPIRED JINGLE POUCH

This fringed woman's pouch is decorated with metal cones (the "jinglers"), a woven beaded strip, and a seed bead rosette that is a variation of the four-pointed morning star. The morning star was an important symbol of courage and purity of spirit for the plains people.

The Comanche tribe ranged from present-day eastern New Mexico, southern Colorado, southern Kansas, Oklahoma, and most of Texas. They were said to be fine horsemen as well as skillful traders. During the 1700's they were "lords of the plains" because of their ability to defend their land from intruders. There may once have been as many as 20,000 Comanches, but today there are about 13,000 members of the tribe. Most live in Oklahoma.

SUPPLIES

- Deer skin, gold
- 90 (approx.) brass cones, ¾"
- Matte seed beads, size 11/0 – Gold, red, green, turquoise
- Nylon beading thread
- Synthetic sinew (for hand sewing)
- Thread
- Heavy-weight interfacing
- Permanent jewel adhesive
- Permanent fabric glue
- Beading loom
- Beading needle
- Leather needle
- Craft knife and straight edge *or* scissors
- Clear tape

Optional: Sewing machine with leather needle

Jinglers or metal jingle cones

INSTRUCTIONS

See pattern on page 30

◆ Cut & Sew:

You can sew this pouch by hand or on a sewing machine.

1. Enlarge the pattern as directed.
2. From deer skin, cut one entire pattern piece (flap, pouch, fringe) plus one pouch. (The pouch-only piece will be the pouch front.)
3. With right sides facing, position the pouch front piece over the pouch back. Sew the front to the back along the side seams *only*. Turn right side out.
4. Topstitch the bottom seam of the pouch.
5. Cut fringe ⅛" wide on the bottom of the pouch and the sides and bottom edge of the flap, using scissors or a craft knife and straight edge.

◆ Bead:

1. Using the beading chart provided as a guide, loom the beaded strip. See "Loom-Woven Beadwork." Adhere tape to the ends of the warp threads. (Photo 1) Cut excess warp threads along the edge of the tape. Fold and glue the taped ends under the loom work.

Continued on page 28

2. Bead the star medallion on heavy interfacing according to the diagram provided. *See "Two-Needle Applique" in the Beadwork Techniques chapter.*

3. Cut interfacing 1/4" larger than the finished medallion all around the beaded design.

◆ **Assemble:**

1. Glue the loomed bead strip on the front of the pouch over the bottom topstitching.

2. Secure the edges of the loom work to the pouch with needle and thread.

3. Turn under the edges of the interfacing around the rosette medallion. Sew or glue the medallion on the flap of the pouch, using the photo as a guide for placement.

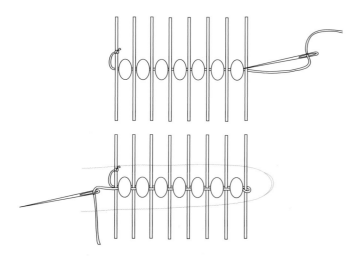

Photo 1 – Place tape over the ends of the warp threads before cutting.

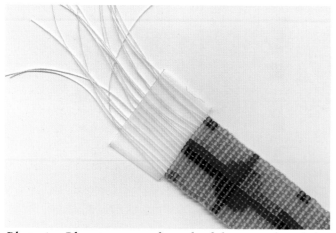

Fig. 1: This shows the looming techniques. See "Loom-Woven Beadwork" section in Beadwork Techniques chapter.

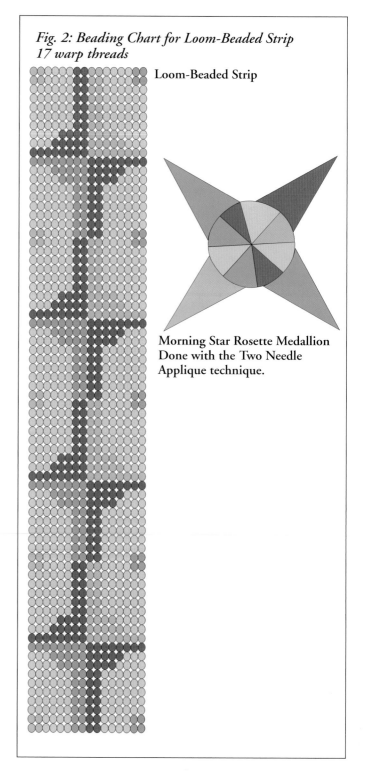

Fig. 2: Beading Chart for Loom-Beaded Strip 17 warp threads

Loom-Beaded Strip

Morning Star Rosette Medallion Done with the Two Needle Applique technique.

Patterns continued on page 30

28

4. To make the strap, cut a 33" x ½" strip of deer skin. Open the pouch flap and glue the ends of the strap inside the open flap. *Option:* Top-stitch each edge of the strap to the pouch flap.

5. To attach the jingle cones, insert a fringe strip through the small end of a cone. Tie a knot in the fringe end. Slide the cone over the knot. Repeat the process to attach the jingle cones to each strip of fringe on the bottom of the pouch. ❏

The metal cone beads were called "jinglers." They were used to decorate clothing, baskets, cradle boards, drums, moccasins, rattles, and pouches. Native American jinglers were cut from tin and shaped around a whit-tled tapered stick. You can buy them at stores and on websites that sell supplies for Native American crafts.

PATTERN

Enlarge 152% for Actual Size

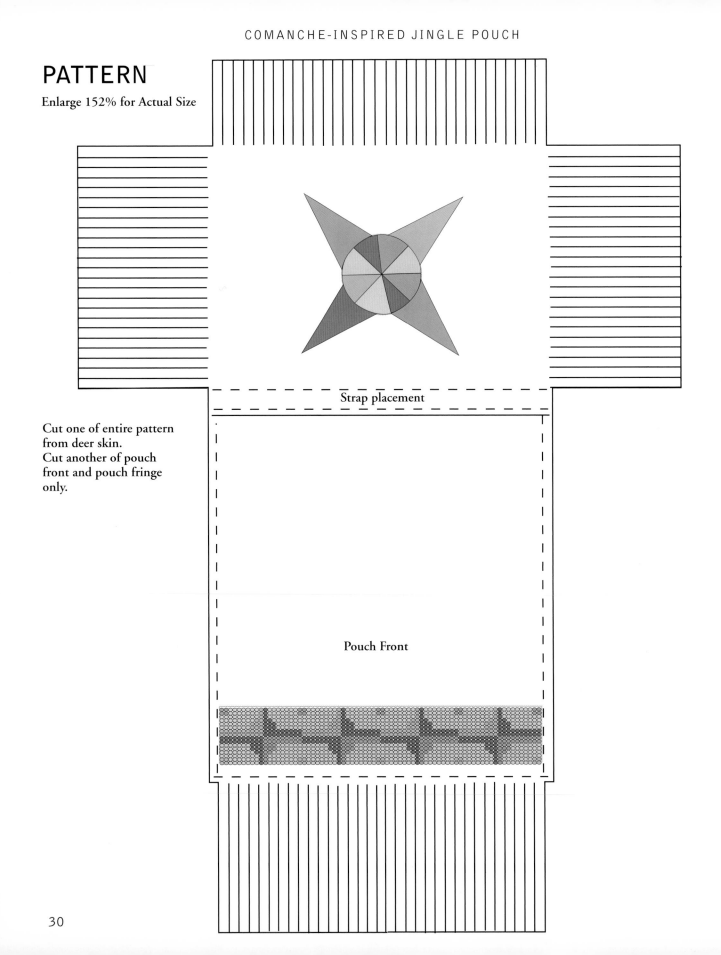

Strap placement

Cut one of entire pattern
from deer skin.
Cut another of pouch
front and pouch fringe
only.

Pouch Front

GREAT LAKES POUCH

Instructions begin on page 32

PATTERNS

Enlarge 115% for
Actual Size

**Front Flap and
Pouch Back**

Add 3" all around
for fringe.

Cut 1 from deer
skin.

Pouch Front

Add 3" to sides and
bottom for fringe.

Cut 1 from deer skin
as shown by arrow.

Braid
fringe
here.

Braid
fringe
here.

GREAT LAKES POUCH

This design is similar to many traditional 19th century floral motifs that Native Americans from the Great Lakes tribes used to decorate their clothing. During that time, Native American embroidery designs were influenced by European immigrants that settled in the area. Tribes around the Great Lakes included people we now call the Chippewa, Fox, Huron, Iroquois, Ottawa, Potawatomi and Sioux.

SUPPLIES

◆ Deer skin, gold
◆ Seed beads, 11/0 matte in the following colors — gold, red, green, turquoise
◆ Beading needles, 2
◆ Beading thread
◆ Synthetic sinew
◆ Leather needle
◆ Transfer paper and stylus
◆ Interfacing, heavy-weight, optional
◆ Permanent adhesive, optional

INSTRUCTIONS

◆ **Sew Bag:**

See pattern on page 31 and Fig. 1 adjacent.

1. Cut pouch front and back from deer skin following the pattern given. Add 3" all around pattern for fringe.
2. With suede side of deer skin facing out, place inside front onto pouch back.
3. Topstitch around pouch sides and bottom curve.

◆ **Two Needle Applique:**

See Fig. 2.

1. Transfer beading pattern to front of pouch.
2. Thread two beading needles with beading thread. Bring needles to front to begin appliqué. Secure thread on back with knot.
3. Thread several beads on one thread.
4. Use the second thread to attach or "appliqué" the strand to the leather every second or third bead.

Optional: Make a beaded applique by sewing beads onto heavy-weight interfacing. Trim edges of interfacing close to beads. Sew or glue applique on pouch flap using permanent adhesive.

◆ **Braided Fringe & Handle:**

(See Photo 1)

1. Cut the margin of leather around the edge of the bag into 1/8" wide fringe.

2. Braid three strands of fringe on each side of flap top. Tie off braid ends with sinew or thread.
3. Cut three 18" x 1/4" lengths deerskin for strap handle. Tie ends together.
4. Braid the strips in a 3-part braid. Tie off braid end.
5. Tie the braided handle strap to braided fringe at pouch flap.
6. Repeat for other side. ❑

Fig. 1

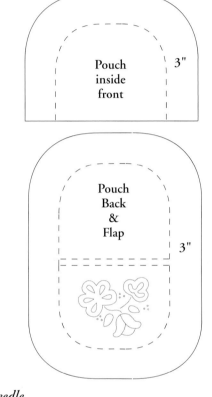

Two Needle Appliqué
Fig. 2

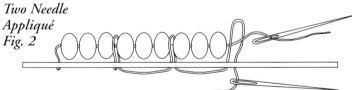

Photo 1: Braid Fringe

Small bags and pouches like this held many items of daily life such as body paint, toiletries, trinkets and sewing materials as well as ceremonial items. Pouches and bags were usually fastened to a belt around the waist or worn around the neck or the wrist. Bags such as this were traditionally made from tanned leather, animal bladders, and all types of furred animal hides from the mole to the bear. As soon as they were available through trade with Europeans, glass beads, buttons, ribbons, and many other materials were quickly adopted by Native Americans to decorate their clothing and bags.

LAKOTA-STYLE PIPE BAG

The Plains Indians were mobile people who moved their belongings on horseback from camp to camp. Indian women created bags and cases of various sizes to hold their possessions and decorated them with beads, fringe, and animal parts. Traditional pipe bags were about 25" long and held the special ceremonial pipe and tobacco. This one is smaller, with fringe on the bottom and one side. It's trimmed with a lane-stitched beaded strip. The top has a beaded fret edging.

The Lakota Sioux Indians were thought to have originally settled in Minnesota, but in the 1700's they migrated into the South Dakota area. The Lakota Sioux occupied a giant piece of land in the plains, which helped to support their bison herds, which they hunted on their land. They were nomadic people who lived in hand made teepees, and hunted buffalo as a source of food, shelter, and warmth. Today the Lakota Indians reside primarily in South and North Dakota. This particular Indian tribe speaks the Lakota language, which is a dialect of the Sioux tribal group.

SUPPLIES

- Deer skin, gold
- Seed beads, size 11/0 – Gold, red, green, blue, white
- Nylon beading thread
- Synthetic sinew (If hand sewing)
- Sewing thread
- Heavy-weight interfacing
- Permanent jewelry adhesive
- Beading needle
- Leather needle
- Craft knife and straight edge

Optional: Sewing machine, computer with scanner and color printer, 1 sheet card stock *or* heavy-weight paper, tape

INSTRUCTIONS

See pattern on page 31.

◆ **Cut & Sew:**

1. Enlarge pattern as directed. Cut pattern on fold from deer skin.
2. With right sides facing and the side fringe pieces tucked inside, sew the side seam. Turn right side out.

Fret Edging

Modern beaders sometimes call this a zipper edging, because the placement of the beads recalls the teeth of a zipper.

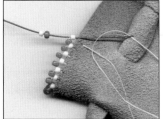

Photo 1

Photo 2

Continued on page 36

3. Sew bottom opening closed.

4. Cut fringe on the side and bottom with a craft knife and straight edge as shown on the pattern.

5. Make slits for the drawstring as shown on the pattern around the top of the bag, using a craft knife.

6. Cut a 36" x ⅜" strip of deer skin for the drawstring. Weave the deer skin drawstring through the slits.

◆ **Bead:**

1. Transfer pattern to heavy-weight interfacing. *Option:* Scan the beading chart artwork into computer. Tape the leading end of a piece of interfacing to a sheet of card stock or heavy-weight paper. Print the actual size beading chart on the interfacing. See Photo 3.

2. Use the **Lane Stitch** to create the design. *See the "Lane Stitch" section in the Beadwork Techniques chapter.* Thread beading needle with beading thread. Knot one end. Bring the needle up from the back of the interfacing. Thread four beads on the needle as shown in the chart. Bring the needle back down through the interfacing. Continue sewing vertical rows of four beads on the interfacing according to the chart. See Photo 4. Knot thread when finished.

3. Trim interfacing edges to 1/4" all around finished bead work. Turn under edges and glue to the back of the bead work.

4. Glue beadwork on pipe bag front, using the project photo as a guide for placement.

5. Edge the top of the bag with red and white seed beads using *"Fret Edging."* See photos 1 and 2 and also the "Fret Edging" section in the Beadwork Techniques chapter. ❑

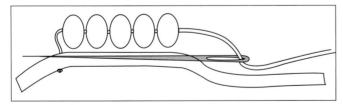

Lane Stitch

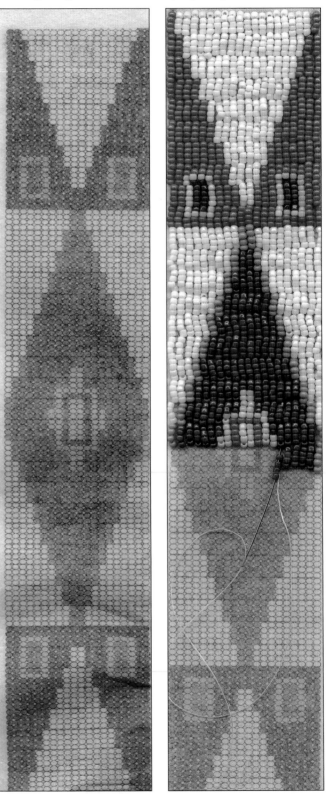

Photo 3 – The beading chart, scanned and printed on interfacing.

Photo 4 – Lane stitching the beads on printed interfacing.

PATTERNS

Leather Pattern

Enlarge 210% for actual size
Cut 1 from deer skin on fold

Beading
Chart
Actual
size

Place on fold.

Turn side fringe
pieces to inside
before sewing
side seam.

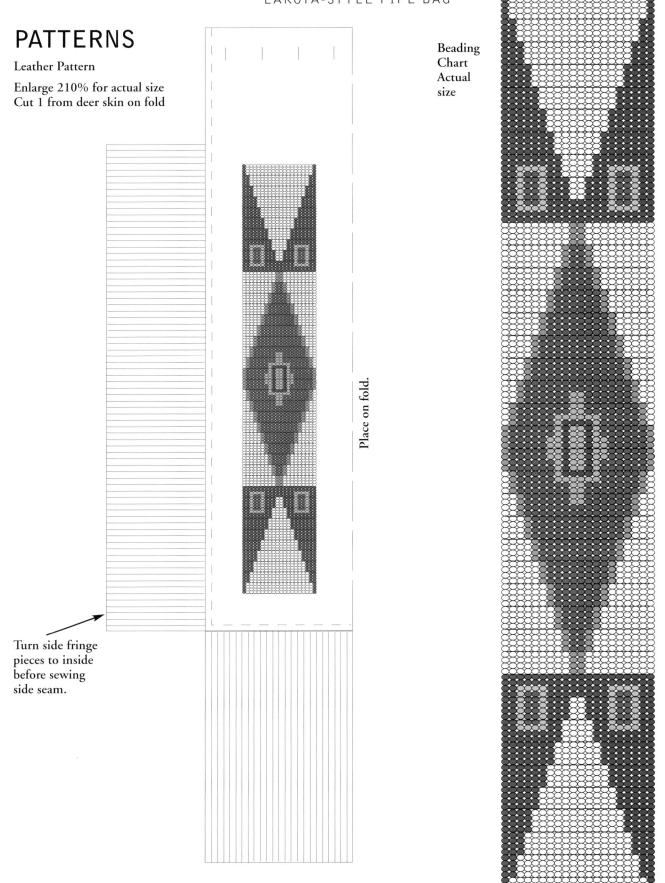

DEER SKIN BAG WITH DIAMOND BEADING

This dramatic bag takes its inspiration from the artistry of the 19th century Comanche, who lived on the southern plains in the area east of the Rocky Mountains. The Native Americans of this time used leather and buckskin to carry a variety of items. The bags were most always decorated with beading or other natural items.

The diamond-motif beaded strip was created on a beading loom, and the flap has a fret edge of yellow beads. Bold graphic designs were often used on looms. Many of the patterns were determined by the size of the loom.

SUPPLIES

- Deer skin, red
- Seed beads, size 11/0 – Red, green, aqua
- Nylon beading thread
- Synthetic sinew (if hand sewing the seams)
- Sewing thread
- Permanent jewelry adhesive
- Leather needle
- Beading needle
- Tension loom
- Leather sewing needle *or* sewing machine with leather needle
- Craft knife and straight edge *or* scissors
- Clear tape

INSTRUCTIONS

◆ **Cut & Sew the Bag:**
See Pattern on page 41.
You can sew the seams of the bag by hand or on a sewing machine.

1. From red deer skin, cut – in one piece – the bag flap, back, and 10" long section for the fringe.
2. Also from red deer skin, cut the bag front and 10" long section for fringe.
3. With suede sides facing, sew the side seams. Turn right side out.
4. Topstitch across the bottom of the bag.

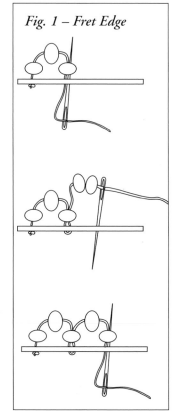

Fig. 1 – Fret Edge

Continued on page 40

5. Cut ⅛" wide strips of fringe on lower 10" sections, using a craft knife and straight edge or scissors.

◆ Make & Attach the Strap:

1. Cut three ⅜" x 20" lengths of deer skin.
2. Align the strips and tie one end together with sinew or thread.
3. Braid the strips to the end to make the strap. Tie off the other end of the braid.
4. Sew each end of the braid inside the bag at the sides of the top. See the pattern for placement.

◆ Bead the Edge of the Flap:

See Fig. 1. This is called a "fret edge." A more modern name is "zipper edge" because the beads resemble the teeth of a zipper. Use yellow seed beads.

1. Thread a beading needle with beading thread. Knot one end. Bring up the needle from the underside of the edge of the flap. Thread three beads on the needle. Bring the needle back through the suede edge leaving a space of one bead from the starting thread. Thread the needle back through the last bead.
2. Add two beads and bring the needle back down.
3. Repeat the process as you work around the flap. When finished, tie off the thread.

◆ Loom the Beaded Strip:

See "Loom-Woven Beadwork" in the Beadwork Techniques chapter.

1. Loom the beaded strip according to the Beading Chart. Adhere tape to the ends of the warp threads near the beads to secure them. Cut the warp threads along the outer edge of the tape. Fold and glue the taped thread ends under the loom work.
2. Glue the loomed strip on the front of the pouch above the fringe and over the topstitching.
3. Sew the edges of the beaded strip to the pouch with a needle and thread. ❑

Fig. 2 – Beading Chart (16 warp threads)

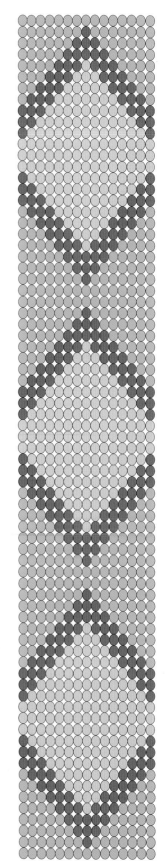

PATTERNS

Enlarge 115% for actual size

Trim edge with beaded zipper edging.

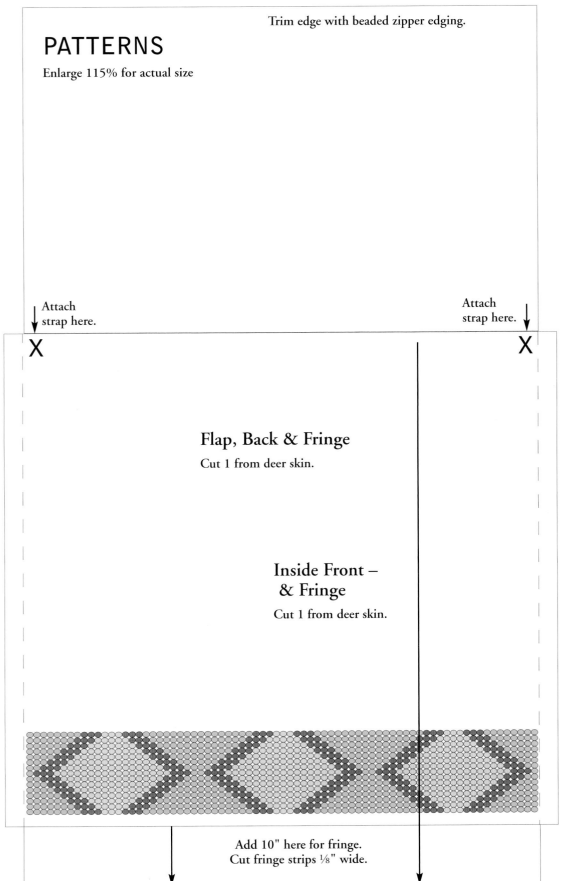

Attach
strap here.

Attach
strap here.

X

X

Flap, Back & Fringe

Cut 1 from deer skin.

**Inside Front —
& Fringe**

Cut 1 from deer skin.

Add 10" here for fringe.
Cut fringe strips ⅛" wide.

BEADED PLACKET ON DENIM SHIRT

The Indians called Chippewa in the United States and Ojibwa in Canada lived in the northern plains. The women wore leather dresses with detachable sleeves and both men and women wore leather capes to protect them from rain and cold weather. The kid skin draped yoke and beaded fringed placket were inspired by Chippewa clothing. The beaded placket is held in place by button covers. If you use hook-and-loop fastener tape or dots, the yoke and beading can be removed so the denim shirt can be washed.

SUPPLIES

- Denim shirt
- Saddle tan doe kid skin
- Seed beads, size 11/0 – Yellow, orange, red, green, turquoise, black, white, dark blue
- Nylon beading thread
- Heavy-weight interfacing
- Permanent jewelry adhesive
- Hook-and-loop fastener tape or dots *or* permanent fabric glue
- 2 button covers
- Beading needle
- Leather needle
- Scissors
- Craft knife
- Straight edge

Button covers are used to attach the beaded placket to the shirt.

INSTRUCTIONS

◆ **Cut the Kid Skin:**

1. Lay the kid skin flat on your work surface. The size of a single kid skin should drape nicely on shoulders. Cut away a panel 1½" x 5" (or the width of the front placket on your shirt x 5") on the center back of the kid skin. See Fig. 1 – Cutting Diagram.

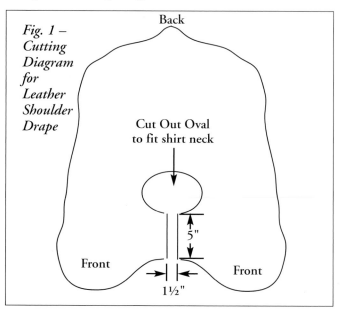

Fig. 1 – Cutting Diagram for Leather Shoulder Drape

Back

Cut Out Oval to fit shirt neck

Front

Front

5"

1½"

Continued on page 44

2. Cut an oval from the skin above the rectangular cutout to fit the neck size of your shirt.

3. Position the kid skin on the shirt, aligning the neck cutout around the base of the collar. Make necessary adjustments, trimming where needed.

4. Use hook-and-loop fasteners or fabric glue to adhere the skin to the shirt along the placket and neck edges.

◆ **Make the Beaded Placket:**

This is done with the Lane Stitch technique, see Beadwork Techniques chapter.

1. Transfer pattern to heavy-weight interfacing.

2. Thread beading needle with beading thread. Knot one end of the thread. Bring the needle up from the back of the interfacing. Thread beads on needle according to the Beading Chart. Bring needle back down through interfacing. Continue sewing horizontal rows of beads on interfacing, following the chart, until the placket design is complete. Knot thread.

3. Trim the edges of the interfacing to 1/4" all around the finished bead work.

4. Turn under the edges of the interfacing and glue to the back of the bead work with fabric glue.

5. Cut a leather strip 2¼" x 12". Glue the beadwork to one end of the strip with fabric adhesive. Let dry.

6. Cut fringe ⅛" wide on the part of the leather strip not covered by the beadwork, using scissors or a craft knife and straight edge.

7. Place two button covers on the top two shirt buttons. Apply jewelry adhesive to the tops of the button covers. Position the beaded placket, centered, on the button covers. Let dry. ❑

Fig. 2 – Beading Chart

SOUTHWEST ROSETTE SHIRT

Beaded flowers in turquoise and coral bloom on the front of a suede shirt. Turquoise, a gemstone of the land, is blue like the sea and the sky. Coral comes from the dried skeletons of sea creatures. Turquoise and coral are two of the four elemental gemstones of the Pueblo Indians. (The others are jet and abalone shell.) Clothing was often decorated with beading that represented designs from nature.

SUPPLIES

◆ Tan suede shirt
◆ 30 (approx.) candy jade teardrop gemstones
◆ 60 (approx.) coral teardrop gemstones
◆ E beads – Silver, orange, turquoise
◆ 6 silver fluted beads, 6mm
◆ Nylon beading thread
◆ Heavy-weight interfacing
◆ Permanent jewelry adhesive
◆ Sewing thread
◆ Beading needle
◆ Scissors

INSTRUCTIONS

1. Using the pattern provided (Fig. 1), cut six circles from heavy-weight interfacing.
2. Arrange the teardrop beads and with a 6mm silver bead in the center make six rosettes – four of coral beads and two of turquoise beads. The beads should touch and cover the interfacing.
3. Glue each rosette on a circle of interfacing. Let dry.
4. Glue the rosettes on the shirt bodice, using the project photo as a guide for placement.
5. Arrange and glue teardrop beads and e beads around the rosettes as shown. Allow glue to dry.
6. Secure the small beads to the shirt with needle and thread. ❏

Fig. 1 – Pattern
Cut 6 from interfacing

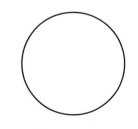

Continued on page 48

CHIPPEWA-INSPIRED BEADED JACKET

Instructions begin on page 50

PATTERN

Beading Pattern for
Chippewa-Inspired
Beaded Jacket

Use the pattern colors
as a guide for the bead colors.

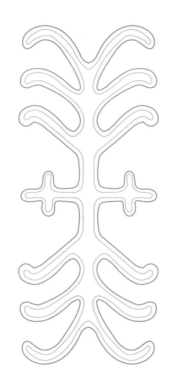

CHIPPEWA-INSPIRED BEADED JACKET

The inspiration for the beaded design on this jacket comes from a Chippewa shoulder bag made between 1820 and 1840. The Chippewa, who lived on the northern plains in the area that is now Minnesota, Michigan, and Canada, were famous for their beaded designs.

SUPPLIES

◆ Ecru jacket

◆ Seed beads, matte finish size 11/0 – Gold, red, turquoise

◆ Nylon beading thread

◆ Beading needle

◆ Tracing paper and pencil

◆ Transfer paper and stylus

INSTRUCTIONS

See page 49 for pattern.

1. Trace the design pattern onto tracing paper. Transfer it to the jacket, using the photo as a guide for placement.

2. Thread a beading needle with beading thread. Knot one thread end.

3. Bring the needle up from the underside of the jacket fabric. Using the pattern as a guide for the bead color, thread three beads on the needle. Bring the needle back down through the fabric. (Fig. 1) Continue beading the design, sewing three beads at a time, until the design is complete. ❏

Closeup

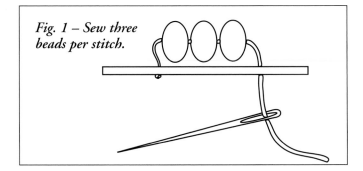

Fig. 1 – Sew three beads per stitch.

BEAR CLAW BEADED SWEATER

Coral teardrop beads are arranged around the neckline of a sweater to represent a bear claw medicine necklace. The Pawnee and other tribes used the claw of the grizzly bear as a sign of great bravery. The claws used for medicine necklaces came from bears killed by a man armed only with a knife – a feat requiring considerable nerve and determination. Bear medicine necklaces were worn for hunting and warfare. The bear claws were sometimes combined with beads, shells, feathers from eagles or hawks, or claws from wild cats or wolverines.

Pawnee Indians are sometimes known as the Paneassa, Pari, or Pariki tribes. The Pawnees could be found along the Platte, Loup, and Republican Rivers of what is now known as Nebraska. They often called themselves "chaticks-si-chaticks," which means "men of men."

SUPPLIES

- ◆ Turquoise sweater
- ◆ 80 (approx.) coral teardrop gemstones
- ◆ E beads – Silver, lime green
- ◆ 6 silver fluted beads, 6mm
- ◆ Nylon beading thread
- ◆ Permanent jewelry adhesive
- ◆ Beading needle

INSTRUCTIONS

◆ Make the "Necklace":

1. Arrange coral teardrop beads around the neckline of the sweater, ½" from edge. Glue in position.
2. Glue a lime e bead above each coral teardrop.
3. Glue a silver e bead between each lime e bead. Allow glue to dry.
4. Secure all the beads with a needle and thread.

◆ Make the Suns & Chevrons:

1. Using the photo as a guide, arrange and glue six groups of four teardrop beads in sun design on the sweater front. Glue a 6mm silver fluted bead in the center of each sun design.
2. Using the photo as a guide, glue lime e beads to form three chevrons under each sun design. Glue a single lime e bead above each sun design.
3. Glue a silver e bead between each chevron. Allow glue to dry.
4. Secure the beads with a needle and thread. ❑

Actual size

THUNDERBIRD CELL PHONE POUCH

The thunderbird figures in the mythology of the northwestern, plains, and northeastern tribes, making it one of the few cross-cultural icons in Native American mythology. The giant bird created the sound of thunder by flapping its wings and carried lightning under its wings. It is a symbol of strength and power.

Wear this pouch on your belt. You can sew the pouch seam by hand or with a sewing machine. Beaded fret edging decorates the flap.

SUPPLIES

- Deer skin, gold
- Seed beads, size 11/0 – White, red, green, yellow, dark aqua, black
- Nylon beading thread
- Synthetic sinew *or* sewing thread
- Heavy-weight interfacing
- Permanent jewelry adhesive
- Beading needle
- Craft knife
- Leather sewing needle *or* sewing machine with leather needle

INSTRUCTIONS

◆ Cut & Sew:
See Pattern on page 57.

1. Using the pattern provided, cut the pouch flap and back piece and the inside front piece from deer skin.
2. With suede sides facing, sew a ⅛" seam around the sides and bottom. Turn right side out.
3. Cut the two slits at the top of the flap so the pouch will slide on a belt.

◆ Bead the Edge of the Flap:
This is called a "fret edge." See Fig. 1 and Photos 1 & 2. A more modern name is "zipper edge" because the beads resemble the teeth of a zipper. Use red and white seed beads.

1. Thread a beading needle with beading thread. Knot one end. Bring up the needle from the underside of the edge of the flap. Thread three beads – one white, one red, one white – on the needle. Bring the needle back through the suede edge leaving a space of one bead from the starting thread. Thread the needle back through the last (white) bead.
2. Add two beads – one red, one white (Photo 1) – and bring the needle back down.

Continued on page 56

3. Repeat the process as you work around the flap. When finished, tie off the thread.

◆ **Bead & Attach the Thunderbird:**

The beaded thunderbird is created with the Lane Stitch technique. See the Beadwork Techniques chapter for more information on this stitch.

1. Transfer the beading pattern to heavy-weight interfacing.

2. Thread beading needle with beading thread. Knot one end. Bring needle up from the back of the interfacing. Thread beads on needle according to chart – no more than five at a time. Bring the needle back down through the interfacing. Continue sewing horizontal rows of beads on interfacing according to chart.

3. Trim interfacing edges to 1/4" all around finished beadwork. Turn edges under and glue to back of bead work.

4. Glue beadwork on pouch front. ❑

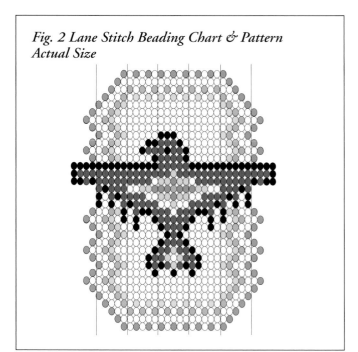

Fig. 2 Lane Stitch Beading Chart & Pattern Actual Size

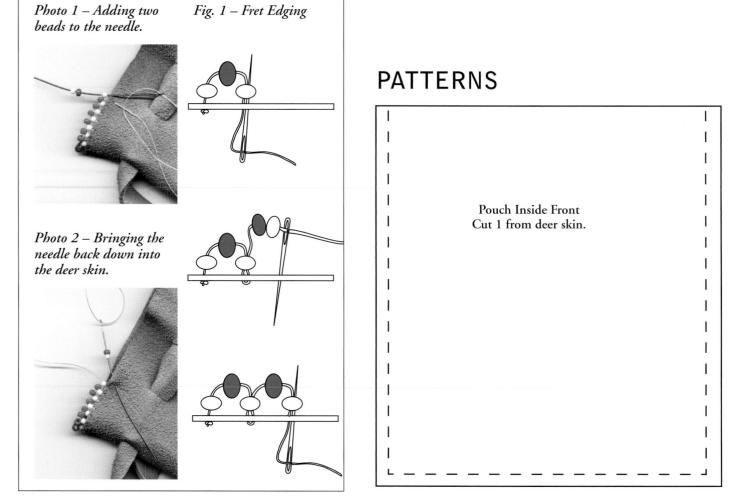

Photo 1 – Adding two beads to the needle.

Fig. 1 – Fret Edging

Photo 2 – Bringing the needle back down into the deer skin.

PATTERNS

Pouch Inside Front
Cut 1 from deer skin.

PATTERNS

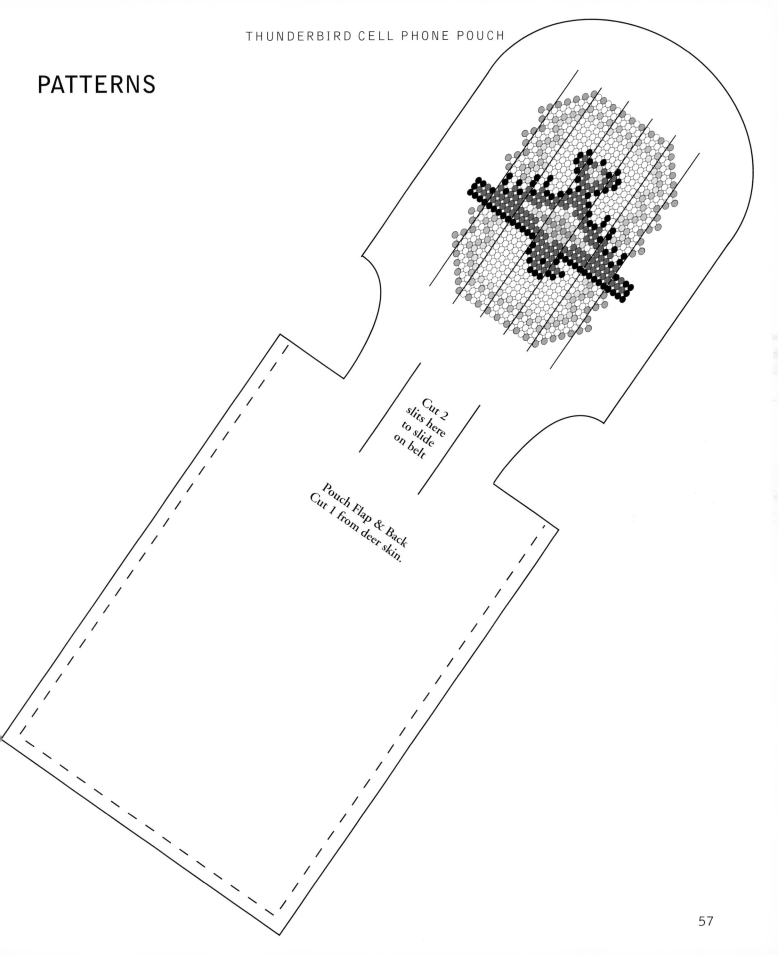

Cut 2
slits here
to slide
on belt

Pouch Flap & Back
Cut 1 from deer skin.

PARAFLECHE

This carrying case, inspired by the parafleche (pronounced "parflesh") of the Plains Indians, is made from hardened rawhide. Smaller cases, like this one, were used to store meats. Larger parafleches were designed to carry clothes. They were made in different sizes but usually in pairs so they could be carried on each side of a horse's saddle. You could use this one to carry valuables, hold a small pack of tissues, or to wrap a small gift. Paints made from charcoal or plant pigments mixed with grease were used to decorate parafleches. Red, blue, green, yellow, black, and brown were traditional colors. Liquid dyes, used here for the painted designs, provide the transparent look of grease paint.

SUPPLIES

- Goat rawhide
- Liquid dyes *or* fabric dyes – Yellow, red, green, black
- Synthetic sinew *or* leather lacing
- Liner brush
- ⅛" hole punch
- Scissors
- Tracing paper and pencil
- Transfer paper *or* light box
- Stylus
- Straight edge

INSTRUCTIONS

1. Trace the pattern and transfer to the rawhide, using transfer paper or a light table to trace over a copy of the design.
2. Score along the fold lines, using a stylus and straight edge.
3. Using the dyes, paint the design on the rawhide. Allow to dry.
4. Punch ⅛" holes in rawhide as marked on the pattern.
5. Fold the long sides to the center and secure with sinew or lacing. Fold the short ends to center and secure. See Fig. 1 – Folding Diagram. ❏

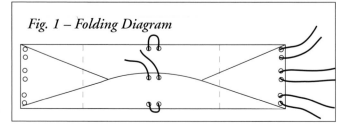

Fig. 1 – Folding Diagram

PATTERN

Enlarge 108% for actual size

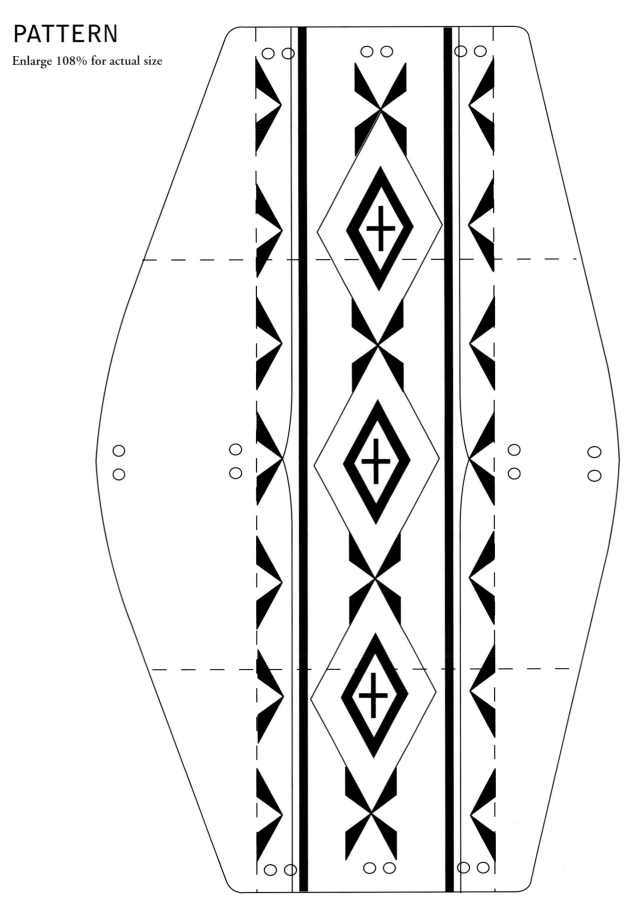

FEATHER SYMBOL BEADED GOURD POT

BY CINDY LEE

This little pot, made from a gourd, has a beaded motif stitched around the outside of the gourd. It's an easy technique that's adaptable to any number of designs. The design around the top is a feather design. Feathers symbolize the creative force. Circular arrangements of feathers, which are related to the sun and the creator, are found on pottery, regalia, and prayer fans.

I used opaque size 11 seed beads to create the beaded designs. Japanese seed beads, such as Delicas, that are uniform in size work well.

The Basics

You can use any size gourd to make this pot, but a small, nicely shaped gourd about 5" in diameter is a good choice. Wear a dust mask during cutting and sanding to protect your mouth and nose.

◆ Preparing the Gourd Pot:

1. With a pencil, mark where you would like to cut the opening. TIP: You will be stitching from the inside to the outside of the gourd – make sure your pot's opening will accommodate your fingers for stitching.

2. With a small saw, carefully cut the gourd at the pencil line.

3. Remove the dried pulp and seeds – they will come out easily if you soak the pot for a few minutes in warm water. Scrub the mold off the skin with a stainless steel pot scrubber, and use a grapefruit spoon to scrape out the pulp on the inside. Let dry thoroughly.

4. Sand the rim smooth and even.

5. *Option:* Sand the inside. Paint with polyurethane or an acrylic paint.

6. Finish the outside of the pot as you like. For a natural look, use a honey maple wood stain followed by a thin coat of semi-gloss polyurethane.

SUPPLIES

- ◆ Gourd pot, 4½ to 5" in diameter, cleaned with finished exterior (See "The Basics.")
- ◆ 1½ yds. artificial sinew, split into 5 threads
- ◆ Seed beads, size 11/0

  ½ tsp. dark red

  ½ tsp. turquoise

  1 tbsp. light orange
- ◆ 3 turquoise beads
- ◆ Beading needle
- ◆ Hand drill with small bit *or* T-pin
- ◆ Pencil
- ◆ Tape measure
- ◆ White glue

◆ How Many Beads?

The projects in this section state how many beads of each color you'll need for the size pot suggested, measured in teaspoons and tablespoons. However, if you use a different-size pot or wish to alter the design, here's a method for calculating how many beads you'll need that provides a generous estimate.

1. Measure the circumference of the gourd at the bottommost line of the design. Example: For this feather pot, the circumference is 13½", and there's a stitch every ⅛". 8 (number of stitches per inch) x 13.5 (the circumference) = 108 lines.

2. Measure the distance from the rim to the bottom of the design. Example: The feather pot measures 2⅜" from the rim to the longest point of the design. 2⅜" (length) x 108 (number of lines) = 256½" (the total length of the design around the gourd).

3. There are about 16 Japanese seed beads (they're slightly smaller than other seed beads) per strung inch. You'll need 4,104 beads – 256½ (total length) x 16 (beads per inch).

4. Beads are generally sold by the gram, with about 190 beads per gram. 4,104 (number of beads) divided by 190 (beads per gram) = 21.6 (number of grams of beads). Round up to 22 grams, and you'll have more than enough.

◆ Using Artificial Sinew:

For stringing and stitching, use artificial sinew in any color. It is extremely strong so it helps avoid the heartbreak of a broken string while you work.

Use a beading needle with a large eye for stitching with this sinew. Split the sinew into five strings by cutting a yard and a half of sinew. Fold it in the middle and gently separate and pull five pieces from this length. *See Photo 1.*

Photo 1 – Sinew split into 5 strands.

◆ Mark the Gourd:

1. Using a pencil, scribe a mark around the prepared gourd about one-third of the way down from the rim. Scribe another line about 1/4" above the first line.

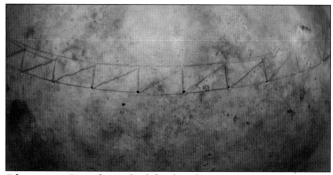

Photo 2 – Gourd marked for beading.

2. Measure the circumference of the gourd at the lower line. Mark as evenly as possible every ½". Note: This gourd's circumference is 12½" so it will have 25 marks. Gourds rarely measure out so evenly – adjust your marks to make them as equidistant as possible.
3. Make rectangles between the two lines by drawing diagonal lines from the bottom marks to the higher line from lower left corner to the upper right corner. This provides the baseline for the stylized feather design. *See Photo 2.*

◆ Make the Holes:

1. Use a small hand drill, a T-pin, or a tack to make the holes for sewing, drilling or poking holes ⅛" apart at the bottom of each vertical line. Make sure the holes go completely through the gourd.
2. Poke four holes about ⅛" apart along each diagonal line, working from the bottom hole.
3. Erase the pencil lines.

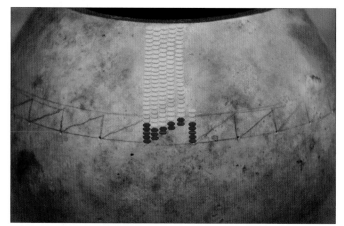

Photo 3. The beaded design.

◆ Stitch the Design:

1. Thread a needle with sinew. Tie a bead on the end, leaving a tail 5" to 6" long (this is for tying off at the end).
2. Starting from the inside, run the sinew through one of the holes at the bottom line. (The attached bead will stop your thread.)
3. Stitch lines of beads, as shown in Photo 3, starting with 5 red beads, 2 turquoise beads, and light orange beads to the rim. Bring the sinew over the rim and inside the gourd. Come out at the next hole in the pattern.
   • If you have trouble finding the hole from inside the gourd, poke a straight pin from the outside through the hole. Use the pin as a guide for your needle.
   • Keep your beaded lines snug by pulling the thread straight out from the next hole (Photo 4). If you pull at an angle, the sinew can cut into the gourd.
   • When you're ready to start a new sinew, bead a line and securely tie on a new piece of sinew so the knot will fall inside the gourd.
4. When you've beaded the entire design, bring the sinew through to the front at the bottom of the previous beaded line. Run the sinew through the stitched beads. This will hold the sinew securely while you tightly tie the end of the sinew to the tail you left at the beginning.
5. Spread a coat of white glue over the rim to hold the sinew pieces in place. Let dry.
6. On another piece of sinew, string the turquoise beads in a cluster, using a turquoise seed bead on one end of each larger turquoise bead. Using the project photo as a guide, work the sinew under one of the beaded lines and tie the sinew to it to attach the beads and create a focal point. ❑

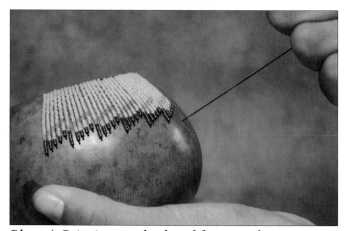

Photo 4. Bringing out the thread for a new line.

ARROW SYMBOL BEADED GOURD POT

BY CINDY LEE

Arrow symbols are powerful indicators of direction, movement, and force. This stitched design of overlapping triangular arrow shapes is similar to the Feather Symbol Bowl. For this design, you may need to reduce the number of lines occasionally to accommodate the curvature of the gourd.

Instructions begin on page 64.

See photo on page 63

SUPPLIES

- ◆ Gourd pot, 4½" to 5" in diameter, cleaned with finished exterior (See "The Basics.")

- ◆ 1½ yds. artificial sinew, split into 5 threads

- ◆ Seed beads, size 11/0

  1 tbsp. turquoise

  ½ tsp. black

  ½ tsp. orange

- ◆ Silver lizard charm

- ◆ Beading needle

- ◆ Hand drill with small bit *or* T-pin

- ◆ Pencil

- ◆ Tape measure

- ◆ White glue

- ◆ Compass

- ◆ Ruler

- ◆ Sturdy paper

- ◆ Scissors

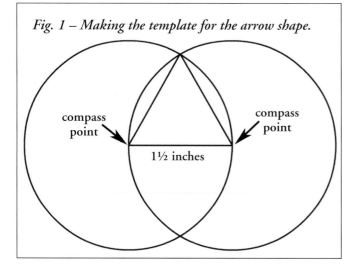

Fig. 1 – Making the template for the arrow shape.

compass point

compass point

1½ inches

INSTRUCTIONS

- ◆ **Make the Template & Mark the Gourd:**

1. Using a pencil, scribe a mark around the prepared gourd not more than one-third of the way down from the rim. Measure the circumference of the gourd at this line. (This gourd measured 13¾".)

2. Divide and mark this line into 9 equidistant points (about every 1½"), adjusting the measurement as needed to accommodate your gourd.

3. Make a paper template for the triangle using a ruler and compass. See Fig. 1. (Use the measurement from step 2 to determine the size of the triangle.) Cut out the template with scissors. Mark dots on the edge of the template for the thread holes at least ⅛" apart.

4. Holding the template with the point of the template on the point marks on the gourd, trace around the template to make the arrow design all the way around. (At the rim of the gourd, the bases of the triangle shapes will overlap, which is what you want. See Photo 1.) Also mark along the arrow shape where you will make the holes for stitching.

Photo 1 – Using the template to mark the arrow shapes and the holes.

- ◆ **Make the Holes:**

1. Make the holes for stitching, using a hand drill with a small bit, a T-pin, or a tack. Make sure the holes go all the way through the gourd.

2. Erase the pencil marks.

◆ Stitch the Design:

1. Thread a needle with sinew. Tie a bead on the end, leaving a tail 5" to 6" long (this is for tying off at the end).

2. Starting from the inside, run the sinew through one of the holes at the point of an arrow shape. (The attached bead will stop your thread. See Photo 2.)

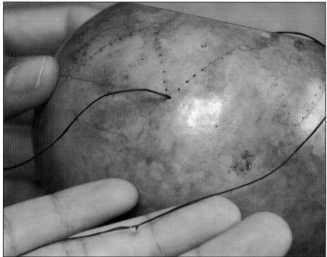

Photo 2 – Coming through the first hole.

3. Stitch lines of beads, as shown in Photo 3, starting with 2 black beads, 1 orange bead, and turquoise beads to the rim. Bring the sinew over the rim and inside the gourd. Come out at the next hole in the pattern.

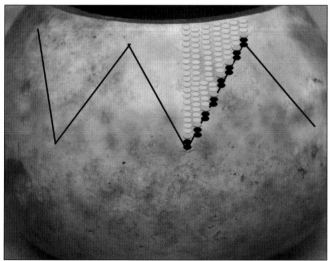

Photo 3 – The beading pattern. (The arrow shapes are marked in black to make them easier to see in the photo.)

• If you have trouble finding the hole from inside the gourd, poke a straight pin from the outside through the hole. Use the pin as a guide for your needle.

• Keep your beaded lines snug by pulling the thread straight out from the next hole. If you pull at an angle, the sinew can cut into the gourd.

• When you're ready to start a new piece of sinew, bead a line and securely tie on a new piece of sinew so the knot will fall inside the gourd.

• In this design, the lines of beads can become crowded at the rim of the pot because of the contours of the pot. The way to keep the lines close together but not too crowded is to reduce the number of lines at the rim on both sides of each triangle. Here's how: String the 2 black beads and an orange bead. Add turquoise beads until the line is a little less than halfway to the rim, then run the thread through the bead line to the left. (Photo 4) Pull snugly.

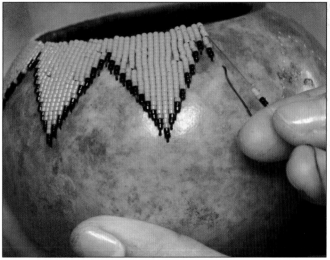

Photo 4 – The beading technique for reducing the number of lines of sinew at the rim.

4. When you've beaded the entire design, bring the sinew through to the front at the bottom of the next beaded line. Run the sinew through the stitched beads. This will hold the sinew securely while you tightly tie the end of the sinew to the tail you left at the beginning.

5. Spread a coat of white glue over the rim to hold the sinew pieces in place. Let dry.

6. On another piece of sinew, string the charm. Using the project photo as a guide for placement, work the sinew under one of the short beaded lines near the rim of the pot. Tie the sinew to secure the charm. ❑

ZUNI BEAR BEADED BOWL

BY CINDY LEE

Beadwork inlaid in a small gourd bowl is an old and colorful tradition of the Huichol Indians of the Sierra Madre. Originally created with colorful stones and shells, these small-scale mosaics were intended as offerings to the gods or containers for good spirits. These modern versions have mosaics made with seed beads inlaid in beading wax. If you've done counted cross stitch, you'll find this square grid pattern very easy to follow.

Bear motifs are symbols of physical strength and leadership.

Beaded Bowl Basics

A beaded bowl project starts with a small (about 4" in diameter), fairly symmetrical gourd. Wear a dust mask during cutting and sanding to protect your mouth and nose.

Preparing the Gourd Bowl:

1. Mark a line on the gourd with a pencil at the place where you would like to cut the gourd to create a shallow bowl. (Photo 1)

Photo 1 – Marking a cutting line on a gourd.

2. With a small saw, carefully cut the gourd at the pencil line.
3. Use a grapefruit spoon to remove the dried pulp and seeds. (They will come out easily when you soak the bowl for a few minutes in warm water. (Photo 2)

Photo 2 – The cut gourd with the seeds and pulp removed.

4. Scrub the mold off the skin with a stainless steel pot scrubber. Let dry completely.
5. Sand the rim until it is smooth and even, and sand the interior so the wax will adhere securely.

6. Finish the outside of the bowl as you like. For a natural look, use a honey maple wood stain followed by a thin coat of semi-gloss polyurethane. (This will allow you to easily wipe off waxy fingerprints later.)

Supplies for Beading:

- Wax – The inlay material is a mix of beeswax and copal (pine resin), which keeps the mixture sticky and prevents the beeswax from hardening and rejecting the beads over time. A beading wax mixture, such as Beadswax[r], which is available online and through several gourd craft suppliers, is already mixed and easy to use.

- Beads – For a nice, even design, use size 11 Japanese seed beads, such as Delicas. The opaque ones come in brilliant colors. For a generous estimate of total beads needed for a 4" diameter bowl, remember a 4" square is 16 square inches. There are approximately 12 size 11 Japanese seed beads in a linear inch, and 144 per square inch. Beads are generally sold in grams. There are about 190 beads per gram, and 28 grams per tablespoon.

- Placement Tool – You can use any size beading needle for inlaying beads. The needle will be easier to handle if you create a tool by cutting a 4" piece of wooden dowel. Using a push pin or small drill bit, make a hole in the center at one end of the dowel. Glue your needle into the hole to make a tool with a handy handle.

- Patterns – There are two commonly used grid patterns for this kind of bead inlay, a square graph (similar to what's used for cross stitch) and a honeycomb graph, which is worked in a circular or diagonal path. The Zuni Bear Bowl is a square graph grid; the Thunderbird Bowl pattern is a honeycomb graph. (Remember your bowl is a creation of Mother Nature who generally laughs at straight lines and perfect circles!) You can obtain blank grids for future projects and download them for free on the Internet. The Bear Paw Beaded Bowl is made without a grid pattern – instead, the design outlines are etched in the wax.

Displaying & Cleaning Beaded Bowls:

Temperatures above 90 degrees F. will cause the wax to soften, and the beads could become dislodged. Do not display the bowl in direct sunlight. If your bowl requires more than a light dusting, it can be cleaned with a swish of cool, soapy water. Allow to air dry.

Continued on page 68

SUPPLIES

- ◆ Gourd bowl, 3½" to 4" in diameter, cleaned with a finished exterior (See "Beaded Bowl Basics.")
- ◆ Beading needle
- ◆ Beading wax mixture
- ◆ Seed beads, size 11/0

  1 tsp. turquoise

  1 tsp. black

  ½ tsp. red

  1 tsp. dark orange

  2 tsp. light orange

- ◆ Orange oil furniture polish
- ◆ Paper towels
- ◆ Knife (for cutting the wax)
- ◆ *Optional:* Oil-based polyurethane

INSTRUCTIONS

◆ Prepare the Bowl with Wax:

1. Shave off a piece of the beading wax mixture. Warm the piece by kneading it in your hand until you can flatten it into a thin pancake.
2. Starting in the center, press the wax into the gourd bowl. Continue pressing and spreading with your thumbs, adding wax as necessary, to cover the interior of the bowl with a very thin coat of wax (about half as thick as the diameter of the beads). See Photo 1.

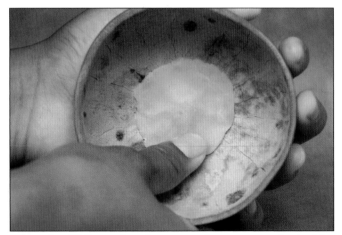

Photo 1 – Using a thumb to press the wax over the inside of the bowl.

3. Before you start beading, remove the sticky wax from your fingers and the outside of your bowl. A spritz of orange oil furniture polish on a paper towel will wipe away the sticky wax.

◆ Add the Beads:

1. Mark the center of the pattern with a yellow bead. (It will help you keep track of where you are.) Lay the yellow bead on the wax – a gentle touch will set it. (You can replace it with a black bead when you're finished.)
2. Follow the pattern, laying beads in a straight line on either side of the yellow center bead to establish the bear and a little of the background color. Do **not** bead all the way to the rim. When you've laid in the center line of the design, continue following the pattern, placing beads directly above or below the line of beads you've established. (Photo 2) After a few lines you will see your pattern emerge. (Photo 3) As you work up the sides of the bowl the curve will make it harder to maintain the linear pattern. That's okay; don't worry.

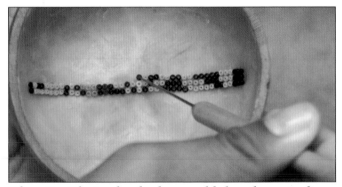

Photo 2 – Placing beads above and below the center line.

Photo 3 – The pattern begins to emerge.

3. Place a line of red beads around the top at the rim.
4. Place a line of dark orange beads below the red beads. (Photo 4) Depending on the depth of your bowl, you may want to make several lines of light orange beads around the rim. The turquoise arrows make an interesting border when interspersed with the light orange beads. Continue placing beads in rows until you have almost reached the bear motif. (Photo 5)

Photo 5 – The two parts of the design – the bear and the rows around the rim – nearly touch.

◆ **Finish:**

1. Spritz some orange oil on a paper towel and wipe away excess wax from the exterior and interior of your bowl. Very gently press the beads as you wipe over them to seat them all evenly.

2. *Option:* Brush a coat of oil-based polyurethane over the beads to help keep them secure. Allow to dry completely. (This could take a couple of days.) **Note:** You may not want to apply polyurethane to white or lighter-colored beads, as it adds a golden hue. ❑

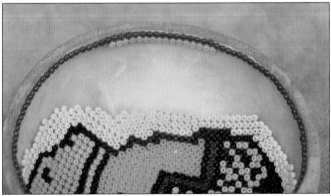

Photo 4 – Placing the first rows just below the rim.

5. When the rim beads and the bear motif are nearly touching, abandon the linear design and neatly fill in the remaining areas. TIP: If you need to fill an odd-shaped little space, lay a bead or two in sideways. This won't disrupt the overall design.

Continued on page 70

GRID PATTERN

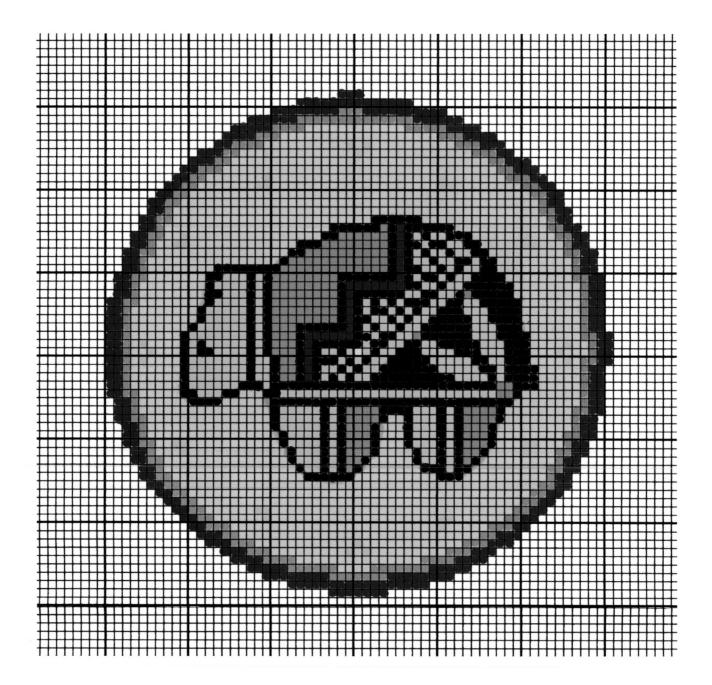

BEAR PAW BEADED BOWL

BY CINDY LEE

This bowl is made with a freeform style of beading. The design is lightly scratched into the wax and the beads are laid in the wax without a grid pattern.

Bear paws are symbols of authority and leadership. Creating a paw motif is a way to summon the power of the animal spirit or indicates the presence of the animal spirit.

Instructions appear on page 72.

See photo on page 71

SUPPLIES

◆ Gourd bowl, 3½" to 4" in diameter, cleaned with a finished exterior (See "Beaded Bowl Basics.")

◆ Beading needle

◆ Beading wax mixture

◆ Seed beads, size 11/0

    ½ tsp. red

    ½ tsp. dark orange

    ½ tsp. medium orange

    ½ tsp. light orange

    ½ tsp. turquoise

    1 tbsp. light yellow

◆ Orange oil furniture polish

◆ Paper towels

Optional: Oil-based polyurethane

INSTRUCTIONS

◆ Prepare the Bowl with Wax:

1. Shave off a piece of the beading wax mixture. Warm the piece by kneading it in your hand until you can flatten it into a thin pancake.

2. Starting in the center, press the wax into the gourd bowl. Continue pressing and spreading with your thumbs, adding wax as necessary, to cover the interior of the bowl with a very thin coat of wax (about half as thick as the diameter of the beads). See Photo 1.

3. Using the pattern provided as a guide, lightly scratch the paw design into the wax with a beading needle. If you need to "erase," rub out the line with your finger and re-scratch until you're happy with the result.

4. Lightly scratch diamond designs around the circumference below the rim, using the photo as a guide for placement.

5. Before you start beading, remove the sticky wax from your fingers and the outside of your bowl. A spritz of orange oil furniture polish on a paper towel will wipe away the sticky wax.

◆ Add the Beads:

1. Lay in the red beads to outline the bear paw design, then add lines of turquoise beads in the areas shown on the pattern. See Photo 1.

2. Fill in the red outline with lines of dark orange, then light orange. TIP: For the smoothest result, lay in beads to follow the lines of the design, then squeeze in beads randomly to fill.

3. Bead the diamond designs, using turquoise, then red, then light yellow, then light orange. (Photo 2, Photo 3)

Photo 1 – The bear paw is outlined.

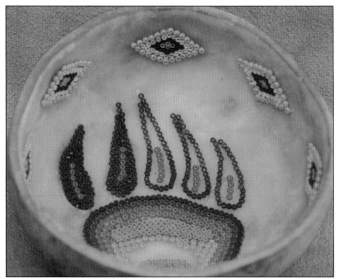

Photo 2 – The diamond designs are added, and the bear paw is beginning to be filled in.

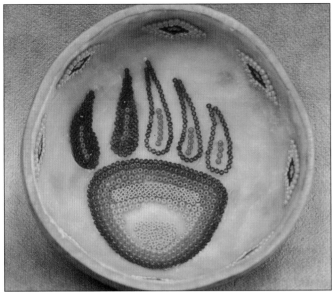

Photo 3 – Another view of the partly completed design.

4. To bead the rim, alternate 3 turquoise beads and 3 light yellow beads. TIP: As you come full circle, you may need to add an extra bead to each color so the pattern will fit evenly.
5. Fill in the areas below the rim around the bear paw motif and the diamonds with light yellow beads.

◆ **Finish:**

1. Spritz some orange oil on a paper towel and wipe away excess wax from the exterior and interior of your bowl. Very gently press the beads as you wipe over them to seat them all evenly.
2. *Option:* Brush a coat of oil-based polyurethane over the beads to help keep them secure. Allow to dry completely. (This could take a couple of days.) **Note:** You may not want to apply polyurethane to white or lighter-colored beads, as it adds a golden hue. ❑

PATTERN

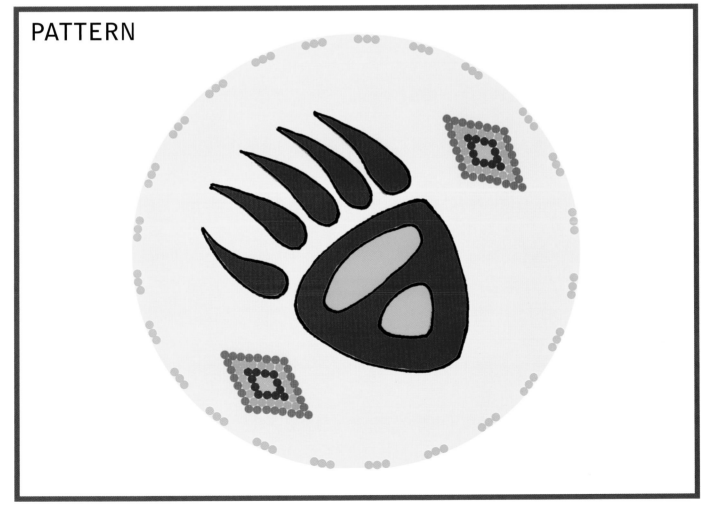

THUNDERBIRD BEADED BOWL

BY CINDY LEE

The thunderbird symbolizes intelligence, power, and wrath. When it flies, the flapping of its enormous wings create thunder. Sheet lightning occurs when it blinks its eyes, and lightning bolts come from the lightning snakes it carries beneath its wings. The thunderbird motif is a fairly small design; it will show well at the bottom of the bowl. But it leaves a lot of rim and background area that needs more interest. As shown in the photo below, there's an arrowhead pattern at the rim and some three-point stars in the background above the bird.

A honeycomb grid is used for the pattern; it's well suited for laying round beads close together. The pattern is worked in a circle from the center that develops into a hexagon.

SUPPLIES

- ◆ Gourd bowl, 3½" to 4" in diameter, cleaned with a finished exterior (See "Beaded Bowl Basics.")
- ◆ Beading needle
- ◆ Beading wax mixture
- ◆ Seed beads, size 11/0

    ½ tsp. turquoise

    ½ tsp. white

    2 tsp. medium blue

    ½ tsp. red

    ½ tsp. dark orange

    ½ tsp. light orange

    1 tsp. yellow

INSTRUCTIONS

◆ Prepare the Bowl with Wax:

1. Shave off a piece of the beading wax mixture. Warm the piece by kneading it in your hand until you can flatten it into a thin pancake.
2. Starting in the center, press the wax into the gourd bowl. Continue pressing and spreading with your thumbs, adding wax as necessary, to cover the interior of the bowl with a very thin coat of wax (about half as thick as the diameter of the beads). See Photo 1.
3. Before you start beading, remove the sticky wax from your fingers and the outside of your bowl. A spritz of orange oil furniture polish on a paper towel will wipe away the sticky wax.

◆ Bead the Design:

1. Lay a turquoise bead in the approximate center of the bowl. Lay a row of turquoise beads all around the center bead. (There will be six beads nestled up against the center bead.)
2. For the next row, nestle a dark orange bead between each

Photo 1 – The center hexagon.

pair of turquoise beads (six beads in all, creating a star shape). Lay another orange bead between each of the star's points to form a hexagon.

3. Following the pattern, continue to lay beads in the hexagon shape of the center. (Photo 1) When the center is well-established, follow the pattern to create the head, tail, and wings. (Photo 2) Lay the beads in diagonal lines or nestle them between beads above or below.

Continued on page 76

Photo 2 – The bird's body and one wing are in place.

4. When the thunderbird and some of the blue background beads are in place, start the rim. Place a line of red beads around the rim, then a line of dark orange, then a line of light yellow.

5. Add light yellow beads, following the pattern, to form downward-pointing arrowheads around the top of the bowl. The arrowhead pattern runs every seven beads, with five beads as the base of the triangle shape and a spacer bead at each end of the base. The arrowhead is built by rows of four beads, then three, then two, and one bead that creates the point. (Photo 3) **Note:** These

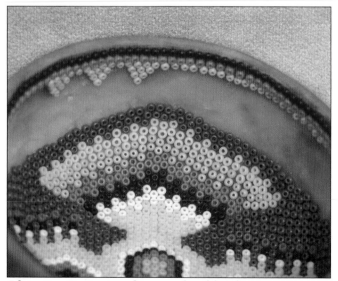

Photo 3 – Beginning the arrowhead border.

types of designs rarely fit evenly around the rim – you may need to add or delete a spacer bead to make the design fit. See Photo 4. (The finished pattern always looks more symmetrical than it really is.)

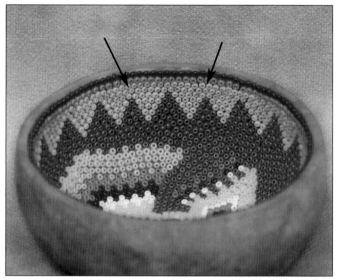

Photo 4 – You may have to add a bead or two here and there so the design will work with the shape and size of the bowl.

6. Add a single row of turquoise beads all the way around.

7. Fill in the areas between the thunderbird and the arrowhead designs with medium blue beads. For variety, add a few three-pointed stars to the background above the thunderbird. (You can see them in the photo that shows the inside of the bowl.)

◆ **Finish:**

1. Spritz some orange oil on a paper towel and wipe away excess wax from the exterior and interior of your bowl. Very gently press the beads as you wipe over them to seat them all evenly.

2. *Option:* Brush a coat of oil-based polyurethane over the beads to help keep them secure. Allow to dry completely. (This could take a couple of days.) **Note:** You may not want to apply polyurethane to white or lighter-colored beads, as it adds a golden hue. ❑

GRID PATTERN

EASTERN WOODLANDS MOCCASINS

Moccasins like these, with soft soles and a puckered center seam, were commonly worn by tribes in the eastern woodlands. In fact, the name of the Great Lakes Ojibway tribe means "people of the puckered moccasin." Well-suited to travel over ground covered with leaves or pine needles, each moccasin is made from a single piece of tanned leather. They are custom made for your foot – you start by making a pattern, using your foot as a template.

SUPPLIES

- Leather (elk, moose or deer hide)
- Leather glover's needle
- Artificial sinew *or* waxed linen thread
- Opaque seed beads, size 11/0 – Light blue, royal, yellow, white, pink, red, light green, dark green
- Beading needle and thread
- Needlenose pliers
- Cutting tools

Pattern-making Supplies:
- 1 sheet copy paper
- Paper for pattern (newspaper or paper grocery bag)
- Pencil
- Scissors

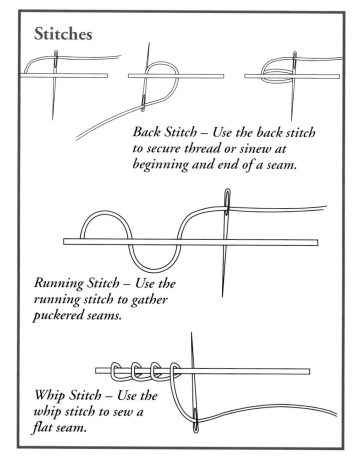

Stitches

Back Stitch – Use the back stitch to secure thread or sinew at beginning and end of a seam.

Running Stitch – Use the running stitch to gather puckered seams.

Whip Stitch – Use the whip stitch to sew a flat seam.

Instructions begin on page 80.

Making a Pattern

1. Place your foot on a piece of copy paper and trace around it with a pencil. Cut out the foot pattern.
2. Fold a brown paper bag or piece of newspaper in half. Position the foot pattern on the paper, with the part of the pattern for the ball of the foot 1/4" from the center fold. Position the heel of the pattern ½" from the center fold and 1¼" from the bottom edge of the paper. See Fig. 1.
3. Draw a straight line across the widest part of your foot. (Fig. 1)
4. Draw an arc on the paper ½" above the toes. (Fig. 1)
5. Mark a point ½" down from end of arc at the widest part of foot. See Fig. 2. Mark another point 1½" from the heel. Draw a line connecting the two points. (Fig. 2)
6. Draw a line 2" from the angled line. See Fig. 3.
7. Draw a cutting line for the heel tab, ½" from the center fold and 1¼" from the bottom edge of the pattern. See Fig. 4.
8. Cut out the paper pattern on the fold. ❑

Fig. 1

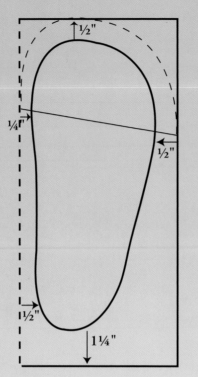

Fig. 2

Fig. 3

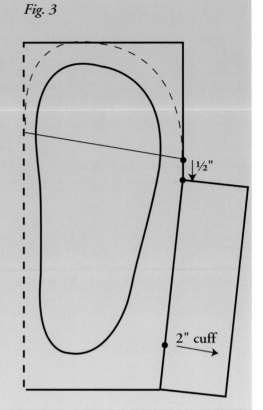

Fig. 4

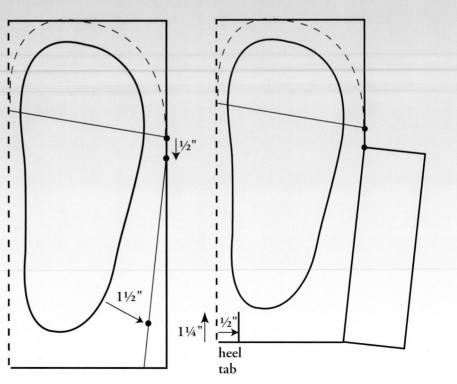

INSTRUCTIONS

◆ Make the Pattern:

Make the pattern for the moccasins, following the "Making a Pattern" instructions, *opposite*.

◆ Cut the Leather:

1. Open the paper pattern. Place the heel area next to the center of the hide (the backbone). See Fig. 5.
2. Trace around the moccasin pattern on the leather.
3. Reverse the pattern. Position on the opposite side of the backbone (Fig. 5) and trace around it.
4. Cut out the leather pieces.

Fig. 5 – The pattern positioned on the hide.

◆ Sew the Moccasin:

Stitch diagrams appear on page 78.

1. Fold the leather with the rough (suede) side out. (Fig. 6) Thread a glover's needle with sinew. Sew a backstitch to secure the sinew. Sew a running stitch from toe to cuff, pulling the gathers as you sew. End with a back stitch.
2. Sew the back seam of the cuff with a whip stitch. Secure with a back stitch.
3. Sew a running stitch along heel, pulling the gathers as you sew. End with a back stitch.
4. Lift the heel tab. See Fig. 7. Whip stitch on the back of the moccasin.

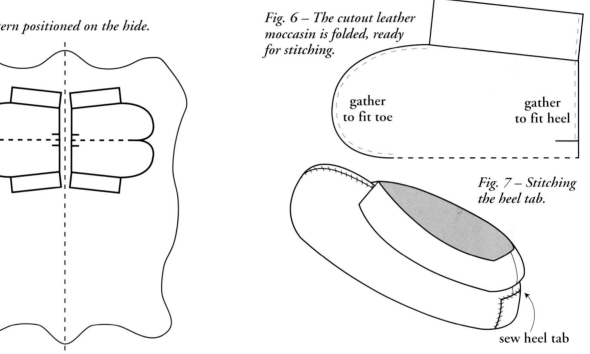

Fig. 6 – The cutout leather moccasin is folded, ready for stitching.

gather to fit toe

gather to fit heel

Fig. 7 – Stitching the heel tab.

sew heel tab

About Moccasins

The word "moccasin" traditionally referred to a low tailored shoe with a puckered U-shaped vamp over the instep. Native American moccasins were designed for the environment of each American tribe. Hard-sole moccasins were intended to protect feet in areas with cactus or sharp rocks. Soft-sole moccasins protected feet from pine needles and cool weather. Moccasin styles are so distinctive that it was possible to tell the wearer's tribe by his footprints or the design of his shoes. Flaps of leather or fur could cover the ankle or be folded down to form cuffs. Different ways of sewing the seams, finishing the heels, and adding decorations like fringe or beading distinguished moccasins. Fringe on the back of plains-style moccasins, for example, may have helped to sweep away footprints.

Moccasins were usually made from soft, tanned hides of buffalo, elk, moose, or deer; rawhide was used to make soles. Thicker hides, while more difficult to sew, lasted longer. Medium thickness leather (3 to 4 oz. weight) is best for making soft-soled moccasins. For best results, lay out the pattern so the pieces go with the grain of the leather. That way, the moccasins will be uniform and less likely to stretch out of shape.

TIP: Make a test pair of moccasins from felt to check the size and fit of the pattern for your foot. Make necessary adjustments to the pattern before cutting your leather.

Continued on page 82.

Bead the Cuffs:

1. Trim the cuff edges with seed beads in a fret edge pattern. See the diagrams, *opposite* for making Fret Edging.

2. Transfer the beading placement pattern to each cuff, using a single line representing the center of each design motif as shown in the Beading Pattern.

3. Thread a beading needle with beading thread. Sew rows of beads to the cuffs, using the Beading Diagram as a guide for color placement and the number of beads. The beading is done using the Lane or "Lazy" Stitch as shown by Fig. 8. See the "Lane Stitch" section in the Beadwork Techniques chapter for more information.

Fig. 8 – How to sew rows of beads.

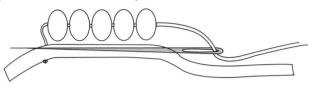

BEADING PLACEMENT PATTERN

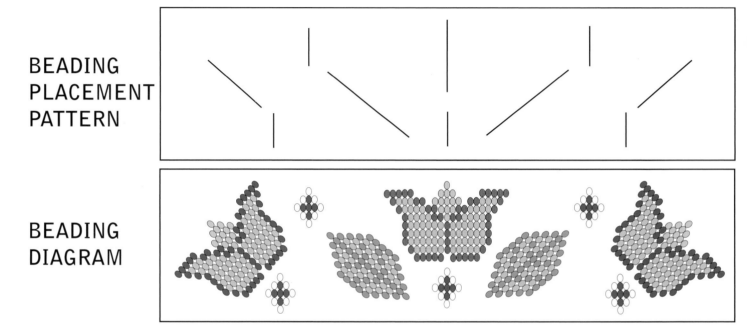

BEADING DIAGRAM

FRET EDGING

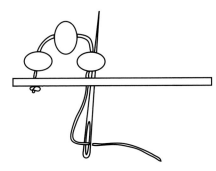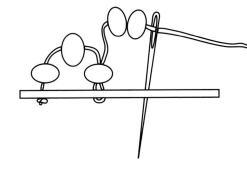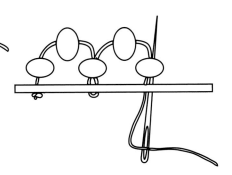

1. Come up from the back side. Thread on three beads. Bring the needle down, then back up through the third bead.

2. Thread on two more beads. Bring the needle down.

3. Bring the needle back up through the last bead. Continue until the entire edge is filled.

GREAT LAKES WOODLANDS MOCCASINS

Instructions begin on page 84.

PATTERN

Actual Size

Beading Pattern for Vamp

WOODLANDS MOCS WITH VAMP

These soft-sole moccasins have a flat, rounded vamp piece over the top of the foot that is hand-stitched on the outside around a gathered toe that is typical of the moccasins worn by a number of tribes in the Great Lakes region. The size and shape of the moccasin is determined by making a tracing of your foot. A beaded design decorates the vamp.

The beading pattern appears on page 83.

SUPPLIES

- Leather (elk, moose, or deer hide)
- Leather glover's needle
- Artificial sinew *or* waxed linen thread
- Opaque seed beads, size 11/0 – Red, dark turquoise, yellow
- Beading needle
- Beading thread
- Needlenose pliers
- Cutting tools

Pattern-making Supplies:
- Paper for pattern (newspaper or paper grocery bag)
- Tracing paper
- Pencil
- Scissors

INSTRUCTIONS

◆ **Make the Basic Pattern:**

1. Trace around your foot on a piece of copy paper to make a template. Draw a line on the template across the widest part of foot.

2. Make a dot 2" above the toes. Make another dot 1½" to the left of the line that marks the widest part of the foot. Make another dot 1½" to the right of the line that marks the widest part. Draw an arc around toe area, connecting dots. See Fig. 1.

3. Make a dot 2" to the left of the heel. Make another dot 2" from the right of the heel. Draw two vertical lines connecting the arc above the toes to the marks at the heels. (Fig. 1)

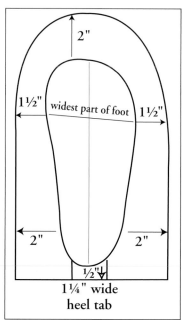

Fig. 1 – Drawing the basic pattern around the foot template.

Continued on page 86

Continued from page 84

4. Draw a horizontal line across the bottom that's ½" below the back of the heel. Mark 1¼" wide heel tab slits at the center bottom as shown in Fig. 1.

◆ **Make the Vamp Pattern:**

1. Place a piece of tracing paper over the basic pattern. Draw a horizontal line 2" below the line marking the widest part of the foot. Draw two vertical lines, straight up from the points where the horizontal line meets the foot outline. See Fig. 2.

2. Round corners evenly at toe. Cut out the vamp pattern. (Fig. 2)

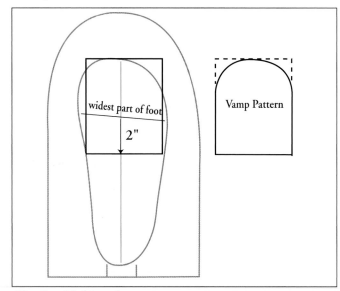

Fig. 2 – Making the vamp pattern.

◆ **Add the Cuffs:**

1. Extend the line across the bottom of the vamp to the edge of the basic pattern on each side. See Fig. 3.

2. Add rectangles 2" wide for cuffs on each side of the basic pattern below the line at the bottom of the vamp. (The arc above that line will be gathered to fit the vamp.) Cut out the pattern.

◆ **Cut the Leather:**

1. Place the basic pattern with the heel section next to the backbone (center) of the hide. Place the vamp pattern as shown in Fig. 4.

2. Trace around the two patterns on the leather.

3. Reverse the patterns and position them on the opposite side of the backbone of the hide. Trace around them.

4. Cut out the four leather pieces.

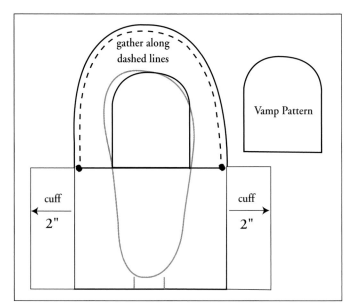

Fig. 3 – Adding the cuffs to the basic pattern.

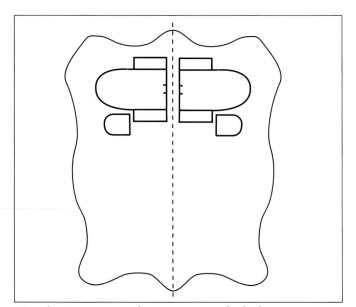

Fig. 4 – Positioning the patterns on the hide.

◆ **Bead the Vamp:**

1. Transfer the Beading Pattern to both vamp pieces.

2. Using the Lane Stitch, sew lines of seed beads to create the design, using a beading needle and thread. To conceal the thread, slide the needle through the leather as shown in Fig. 5. Bring the needle up through the top of the leather. Thread on a row of beads and run the needle through the leather. Continue the process to complete the beaded design, using the project photo and Beading Pattern as guides for the colors and numbers of beads.

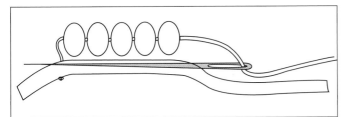

Fig. 5 – Sewing rows of beads.

See "Lane Stitch" section in the Beadwork Techniques chapter for more information.

◆ **Sew the Moccasin:**

1. Fold one leather moccasin piece with the smooth side of the leather to the outside. Thread a glover's needle with sinew.

2. Sew a backstitch at the top of the cuff to secure the thread. Whip stitch from the top of the cuff to the heel tab slit. End with a back stitch. (Fig. 6)

3. Fold up the heel tab. Whip stitch the heel tab to the back

casin. (Fig. 8) Pull the threads to gather the leather to fit the curved part of the vamp piece. Adjust gathers as needed.

5. Whip stitch the vamp to the gathered moccasin. (Fig. 9)

6. Repeat steps 1 though 5 to make the other moccasin. ❑

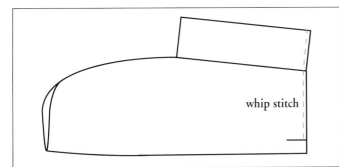

Fig. 6 – Whip stitching the back seam.

of the moccasin. (Fig. 7)

4. Sew 1/4" running stitches around the toe arc of the moc-

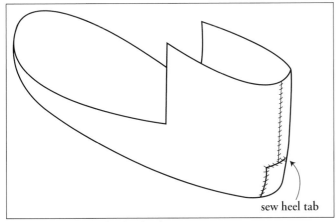

Fig. 7 – Sewing the heel tab.

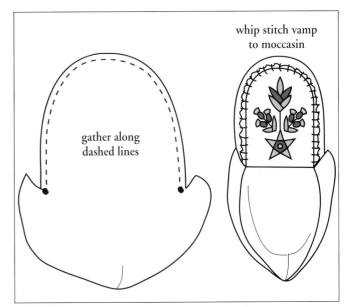

Fig. 8 – Sewing the running stitches for gathering.

Fig. 9 – The vamp is stitched in place.

PLAINS HARD-SOLE MOCCASINS

Hard-soles give moccasins added durability and provide additional protection to the bottoms of the wearer's feet from prairie grass, rocks, and cactus. The soft top, which is cut in one piece, has fold-down cuffs and a back seam finished with fringe. Beaded fret edging finishes the flaps and top edge, and a loomed beaded strip in a diamond pattern decorates the top of each moccasin. The wearer's foot determines the size and shape of the pattern, and the stiff rawhide sole must be punched before stitching.

SUPPLIES

- Leather for upper moccasin (elk, moose, or deer hide)
- Rawhide for moccasin sole
- Awl *or* small leather punch
- Leather glover's needle
- Artificial sinew *or* waxed linen thread
- Opaque seed beads, size 11/0 – Red, yellow, white, royal, turquoise
- Beading loom
- Beading needle
- Beading thread
- Leather contact cement
- Needlenose pliers
- Cutting tools

Pattern-making Supplies:
- Paper for pattern (newspaper or paper grocery bag)
- Tracing paper
- Pencil
- Scissors

INSTRUCTIONS

◆ **Cut the Sole Pieces:**
1. Trace around your foot on a piece of paper. Draw a line ⅛" larger all around. Cut out the pattern.
2. Position the sole pattern on rawhide and trace around it. Reverse the pattern, position it on rawhide, and trace around it. Cut out both pieces.
3. Using an awl, punch stitching holes ⅛" from the edge of each sole and ⅛" apart. See Fig. 1.

◆ **Cut the Upper Moccasin Pieces:**
1. Place one foot on a piece of paper and trace around it. Draw a line across the widest part. See Fig. 2.
2. Make a dot 2" above the toe area. Make a dot 2" from each end of the line marking the widest part. Draw an arc over the toe area, connecting the dots. (Fig. 2)

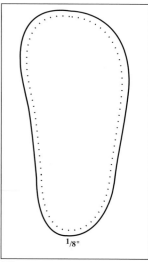

⅛"

Fig. 1

Continued on page 90

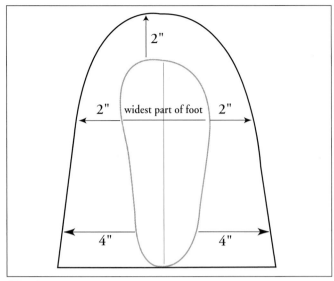

Fig. 2

3. Make a dot 4" from each side of the heel area of the pattern. Draw lines connecting the toe arc to the marks in the heel area. (Fig. 2)

4. Draw a horizontal line across the bottom of the moccasin pattern, even with the back of the heel. (Fig. 2)

5. Mark the center slit by drawing a vertical line from the center of the heel area to the line marking the widest part of the foot. Draw horizontal lines 1¼" long on each side of this center slit marking. See Fig. 3.

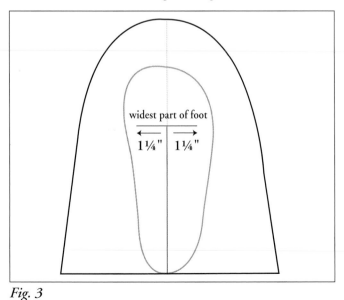

Fig. 3

6. Position the pattern with the heel along the backbone (center) of the hide. Trace around the moccasin pattern on the leather. Reverse the pattern, reposition on the opposite side of the hide along the backbone, and trace around it.

7. Cut out both pieces, and cut along the marked slit lines.

◆ **Sew the Moccasins:**

1. Place an upper moccasin piece – smooth side of the leather up – on one of the sole pieces. Thread a glover's needle with sinew. Beginning at the toe, whip stitch one side of the upper moccasin piece to the rawhide sole, ending the whip stitching at the center back of the heel. See Fig. 4 for a view from the top and Photo 1 for a view from the bottom. (About 2" of leather will extend beyond the stitching at heel.)

2. Whip stitch the other side of the moccasin from toe to heel.

3. Sew a running stitch at the heel from sole to heel top to form the back of the moccasin.

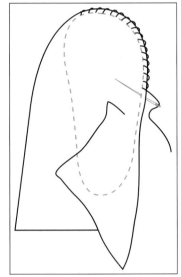

Fig. 4

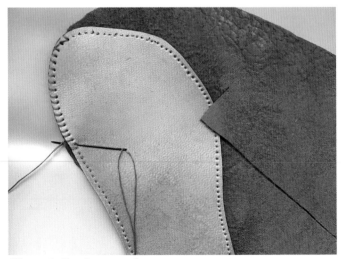

Photo 1: Sewing on sole.

Sew a second running stitch between the first set of running stitches, from heel top to sole. End with a back stitch.

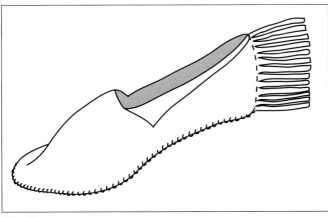

Fig. 5

4. Repeat steps 1 through 3 to stitch the other moccasin.
5. Cut the leather at the back of the heel to make fringe ⅛" wide. See Photo 2.

Photo 2: Fringe on back.

◆ **Bead:**

1. Thread a beading needle with beading thread. Sew beads to make a fret edge with red and white seed beads on both cuffs and the top edge of each moccasin. *See "Fret Edging" at right.*

2. Using a beading loom, loom two beaded strips, each 11 beads wide, according to the Beading Chart. *See "Loom Woven Beadwork" section in the Beadwork Techniques chapter for more information.*

Fret Edging

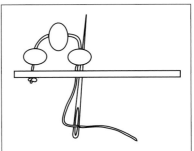

1. Come up from the back side. Thread on three beads. Bring the needle down, then back up through the third bead.

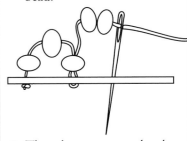

2. Thread on two more beads. Bring the needle down.

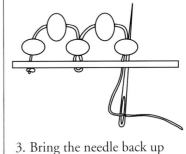

3. Bring the needle back up through the last bead. Continue until the entire edge is filled.

Continued on page 92

Photo 3: Sole of moc.

3. Wrap tape around the warp threads next to outer rows of beads. Cut excess warp threads along the edge of the tape.
4. Fold and glue the taped ends under the loomed strips.
5. Glue a loomed strip to each moccasin as shown in the project photo.
6. Secure the edges of the loomed strips to the moccasins with a beading needle and thread. ❑

Photo 4: Closeup of beaded strip.

Beading Chart

WAR BONNET BROW BAND

The design for this brow band was inspired by the beaded bands used to decorate the elaborate feathered war bonnets that have become emblematic of Plains Indian tribes. The Sioux, Pawnee, and Cherokee Indians decorated their brow bands with beaded geometric designs. The four points on the beaded strip of this band symbolize the four regions of the universe or north, south, east and west. The arrows symbolize force, movement and power.

Instructions appear on page 94.

SUPPLIES

- Elk leather strip, 2½" x 33"
- 2 red leather circles with pinked edges, 2" diameter
- Opaque seed beads, size 11/0 – White, turquoise, royal, red, yellow, green
- Beading thread
- Beading needle
- 2 silver conchos, 1¼"
- 8 aluminum cones, 1⅛" long
- Permanent jewel adhesive
- Beading loom
- Tape measure
- Cutting tools

INSTRUCTIONS

See photo on page 93

- **Make the Beaded Piece:**

1. Warp the beading loom with 32 threads. Using the Beading Chart as a guide, weave a beaded strip. *See Fig. 1 and "Loom-Woven Beadwork" section in the Beadwork Techniques chapter for detailed instructions.*

- **Assemble:**

1. Center and glue the beaded piece on the elk leather strip. Tack the edges of beaded piece to the leather with a beading needle and thread.
2. Measure 7" from each end of the leather strip for the fringe and mark. Make a fret edging with red and white seed beads on the rest of both sides of the leather, leaving the 7" ends unbeaded for fringing. *See Fig. 2 and "Fret Edging" section in the Beadwork Techniques chapter for more details.*
3. Glue one of the red leather circles on each end of the beaded piece.
4. Center a silver concho on each red leather circle and glue in place.
5. Cut two holes through the two layers of leather at the center of each concho, using a craft knife and straight edge.
6. Cut four elk skin strips 16" long and 3/16" wide. Thread two strips through the holes in the center of each concho. Center the strips so the ends are even and tie the strips at the front of the concho.
7. Slip an aluminum cone on the end of each leather strip. On each, knot the end of the leather and slide the cone over the knot.
8. Cut fringe 1/4" wide on each 7" end of the brow band.

To wear: Position the band around your forehead with the beaded strip above your face. Tie the fringe pieces together at the back your head. ❏

Fig. 2 – Fret Edging

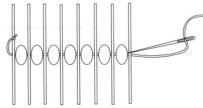

Beading Chart (32 threads)

Fig. 1 – Loom Woven Beadwork

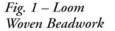

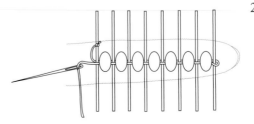

1. Thread a beading needle with about 36" beading thread. Tie the end of the thread to the outer warp thread. Thread the first row of beads on the needle according to the Beading Chart. Bring the threaded row of beads *under* the warp threads on the loom. Press the beads up between the warp threads with your finger.

2. Thread the needle back through the beads, this time passing the thread *over* the warp threads.

LAKOTA-STYLE TURTLE AMULET POUCH

Instructions begin on page 96.

PATTERNS

Beading Chart (Actual Size)

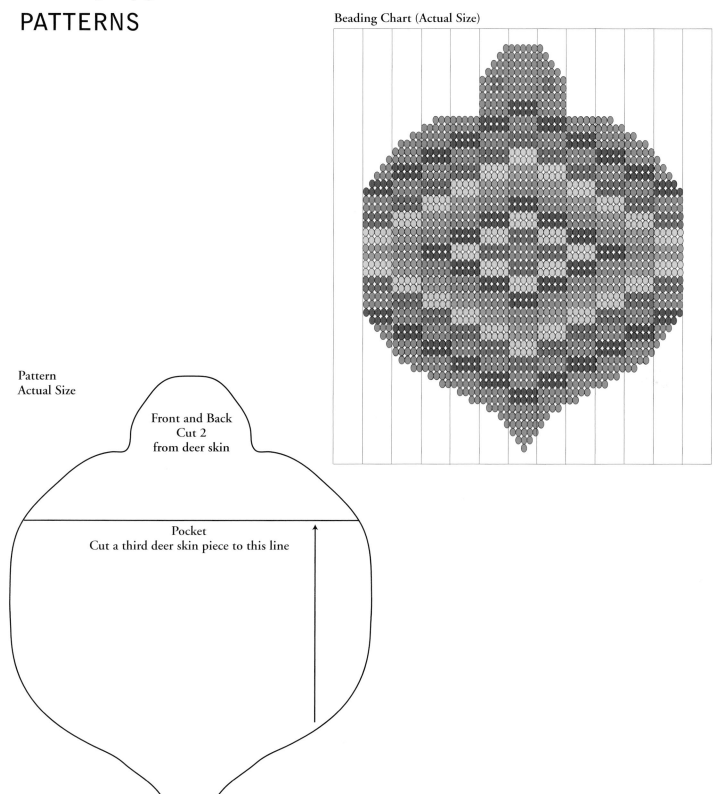

Pattern
Actual Size

Front and Back
Cut 2
from deer skin

Pocket
Cut a third deer skin piece to this line

LAKOTA-STYLE TURTLE AMULET POUCH

Patterns appear on page 95.

The turtle symbolizes strength, feminine power, fertility, perseverance, and long life. Most symbols were developed from what the craftsmen saw around them. Many of nature's gifts took on symbolic meanings and became a part of the art and culture. This symbol was considered to defy death. The Lakota nation is primarily in North and South Dakota where turtles are a natural occurrence. This beaded pouch has a pocket on the back and can be worn from a belt. The finished size is 3½" x 4½". Four turquoise nuggets are used for the turtle's feet.

SUPPLIES

- Deer skin
- Opaque seed beads, size 11/0 – Turquoise, royal blue, yellow, red, green
- Beading thread
- Beading needle
- Glover's leather needle
- Synthetic sinew
- 4 turquoise nuggets, 18mm x 12mm (for the "feet")
- Pencil or water-erase pen
- Tracing paper
- Transfer paper and stylus

INSTRUCTIONS

See pattern on page 95.

◆ Lane Stitch the Beads:

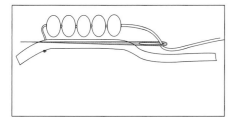

Fig. 1 – Lane Stitch

1. Trace the pattern provided for the turtle shape of the leather and transfer to the smooth side of the deer skin. **Don't** cut out the pieces now.

2. On the transferred pattern on the deer skin that you'd like to be the front of the pouch, draw vertical lines according to the Beading Chart.

3. Thread a beading needle with beading thread. Using the lane stitch, sew rows of five beads between the lines on the leather according to the design shown on the Beading Chart. To conceal the threads as you stitch, run the needle through the thickness of the leather. Knot the beading thread on the back of the leather to secure.

◆ Sew the Pieces Together:

1. Cut out the front piece of the leather (the one with the beading). (It should be 3/16" larger all around than the beaded area.)

2. Cut a second piece of leather the same size. Cut a third piece of leather for back pocket.

3. Stack the pieces this way: Beaded piece (beaded, smooth side up), same-size plain piece (smooth side down), pocket (smooth side facing out).

4. Cut three 7" x ⅛" strips of deer skin. Braid the strips. Bring the ends of the braid together, forming a loop. Tie sinew around the ends.

5. Insert the ends of the braided loop between the two larger leather pieces at the turtle's head. Using a glover's needle and sinew, stitch the loop to the turtle top and wrap the sinew securely around the base of the hanging loop as shown in photo.

6. Using the glover's needle with sinew, whip stitch all three layers of leather together around the edges. Knot sinew to secure. Trim, leaving a tail. Thread the sinew tail back through several stitches. Cut off the excess.

◆ Add the Feet:

1. Thread the beading needle with beading thread. Secure the thread on one side of the leather at one of the points where a foot is to be attached. Thread a turquoise nugget and a turquoise seed bead on the beading needle. Bring the needle around the seed bead, then back through the nugget. Pull the thread taut, bringing the nugget next to the leather pouch. Knot the thread on the leather. Pass the needle back through the nugget, around the seed bead, and back through the nugget. Knot the beading thread on the leather. Bring the beading thread into the leather edge about ½". Trim the thread tail.

2. Repeat step 1 to attach the remaining three turquoise nuggets. ❏

HAIRPIPE CHOKER

"Hairpipe" is the name given to long, tubular beads, 1½" or longer, worn by Indians of the eastern United States since prehistoric times. Archeological evidence documents Indian uses of long, tubular beads in a variety of materials, including bone, shell, and copper before the arrival of Columbus in 1492. Later, tubular beads made of glass, brass, and silver (also referred to as hairpipes) were brought by white traders.

The finished length of this choker is 14¼". To determine your choker size, measure the distance around your neck with a measuring tape. Add 2" for an end clasp or closures. This is the finished size of your choker. To adjust the size, add or delete beads.

SUPPLIES

◆ 8 bone hair pipes, 1½"

◆ 16 bone hair pipes, 1"

◆ 8 bone four-hole spacers

◆ 22 round horn beads, 8mm

◆ 8 round turquoise beads, 8mm

◆ 56 round turquoise beads, 4mm

◆ 11 round brass beads, 2mm

◆ 56 brass heishi, 4mm

◆ Turquoise seed beads

◆ Gold crimp beads

◆ Gold hook and eye clasp, 10mm

◆ Bead stringing wire

◆ Needlenose pliers

INSTRUCTIONS

1. Cut four 25" lengths of bead stringing wire. Bring the four ends together. Thread a crimp bead on the wires. Add one side of the clasp. Pass the ends of the wires back through the crimp bead, leaving 2" tails. Crimp the bead. (Fig. 1)

2. Thread an 8mm horn bead on all the wires and wire tails. (Fig. 2)

3. Separate the wires into two groups. Thread a 2mm round brass bead on each group. (Fig. 3)

4. Separate the wires into four groups. Thread seed beads and 2mm round beads on each group as shown in Fig. 4.

5. Thread the wires and wire tails through a four-hole spacer. Add a 4mm turquoise round bead and a crimp bead on each wire. (Fig. 5) Pull wires taut. Crimp beads. **Note:** The four crimp beads in step 5 keep the end wires with the seed beads and clasp snug and finished, which makes the choker wires more manageable. The four crimp beads could also be replaced with four brass heishi.

6. Add beads on each wire in this order: 1" hair pipe bead, brass heishi, 4mm turquoise round, four-hole spacer, 4mm turquoise round, brass heishi, 1" hair pipe bead, brass heishi, 4mm turquoise round, four-hole spacer, 4mm turquoise round, brass heishi, 8mm horn, 1½" hair pipe, 8mm horn, brass heishi, 4mm turquoise round, four-hole spacer, 4mm turquoise round, brass heishi, 8mm turquoise round, brass heishi. Add an 8mm horn bead at the center.

7. Reverse the order of step 6 and repeat to make the other side of the choker.

8. To attach the other side of the clasp, thread one wire through each hole of the last four-hole spacer bar. Thread a 2mm brass round on each wire. On each of the two outer wires, add five turquoise seed beads. On each of the two middle wires, add two turquoise seed beads. Bring the ends of the wire together. Add a 2mm brass round bead, an 8mm horn, a crimp bead and the other side of the clasp. Thread the wires around the clasp, and pass them back through the crimp bead. Crimp the bead. Thread the wire tails through the 8mm horn bead. Trim the wire tails. ❑

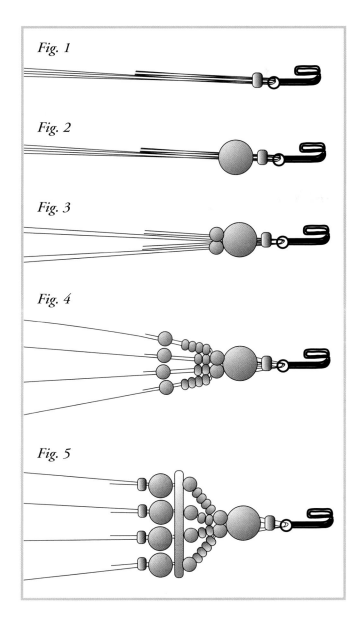

Fig. 1

Fig. 2

Fig. 3

Fig. 4

Fig. 5

HOPI-INSPIRED CORAL & TURQUOISE NECKLACE

The Hopi are among the best-known of the western Indians. Their villages in the Southwestern desert, called pueblos, which date back a thousand years, are the longest continuously occupied dwellings in North America. The Hopi grew corn as a staple crop and it's believed they would have traded corn for the turquoise, coral, and silver beads that were used to make this necklace.

Native Americans of the Southwestern United States believe turquoise connects earth and sky and it is one of their sacred stones. It is one of the four elemental gemstones of Pueblo Indians. (The others are coral, jet, and abalone shell.) Coral was believed to quiet the emotions, bringing peace.

SUPPLIES

◆ 57 turquoise nuggets, 15mm x 10mm

◆ Coral nuggets

◆ 2 silver cone bead caps, 15mm

◆ 120 (approx.) silver round washers, 6mm

◆ 2 silver round beads, 6mm

◆ 6 coral round beads, 4mm

◆ 2 silver crimp beads

◆ Silver hook and eye clasp

◆ .018 bead stringing wire

◆ Needlenose pliers

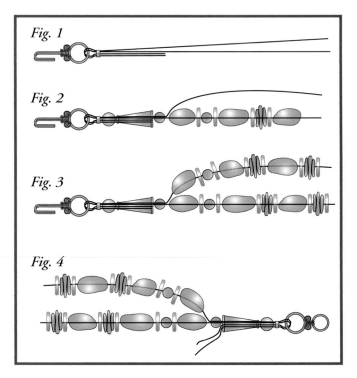

Fig. 1

Fig. 2

Fig. 3

Fig. 4

INSTRUCTIONS

*The finished size of this necklace is 28".
You can add or subtract beads to make a
longer or shorter necklace.*

1. Cut two 35" lengths of bead stringing wire. Hold both wires together at
   one end. Thread a crimp bead on
   both wires. Thread the wire ends
   through the hook side of the clasp,
   then back through the crimp bead,
   leaving a 1" tail. Crimp the bead next
   to the clasp. (Fig. 1)
2. Thread a 6mm silver bead, a cone
   bead cap, and a 4mm coral bead on
   both wires and over the wire tails.
   (Fig. 2)
3. Separate the long wires. On one wire,
   thread a turquoise nugget, a silver
   washer, a 4mm coral bead, and a silver washer.
4. Add the following grouping 28 times:
   a turquoise nugget, a silver washer,
   three coral nuggets, and a silver
   washer.
5. End this strand with a turquoise
   nugget, silver washer, a 4mm coral
   bead, a silver washer, and a turquoise
   nugget. Secure the end of the strand
   with a clamp while you bead the next
   strand.
6. On the second wire, thread a
   turquoise nugget, a silver washer, a
   4mm coral bead, and a silver washer.
   (Fig. 3)
7. Add the following grouping 23 times:
   a turquoise nugget, a silver washer,
   three coral nuggets, and a silver
   washer.
8. End this strand with a turquoise
   nugget, a silver washer, a 4mm coral
   bead, a silver washer, and a turquoise
   nugget.
9. Bring both wire ends together.
   Thread a crimp bead on the ends of
   the wires. Thread the wires through
   the eye side of the clasp, then back
   through the crimp bead, the 6mm silver bead, and the cone bead cap. Pull
   wires taut. Crimp the bead. (Fig. 4)
   Cut the wire tails. ❏

WAMPUM CHOKER

The word "Wampum" comes from the Narragansett word for white shell beads. Wampum beads are made of shell – white ones from whelk shell and purple-black ones from the growth rings of the shell of the Northern Quahog, a hard shell clam. Native-made wampum was strung and used as currency. Its distinctive shape and color made it difficult to counterfeit, although attempts at imitations included beads of stone and other materials. Wampum beads are cylindrical and the shell pieces are drilled lengthwise, a more difficult process than drilling from top to bottom.

The finished length of this necklace is 14". To determine the proper size for you, measure the distance around your neck with a measuring tape. Add 2" for the clasp. This is the finished size of your choker. Add or subtract rows of beads to adjust the size to fit.

SUPPLIES

◆ 4½ yds. round leather lace, 1mm

◆ 3-4 strands, 23" long, of shell tube beads, 4mm-5mm

◆ Metal clasp with 15mm hook and 10mm eye

◆ Buck skin scraps (for spacers)

◆ Beading thread

◆ Beading needle

◆ Artificial sinew

◆ Beading loom

◆ Leather punch

◆ Large eye needle

◆ Tape measure

INSTRUCTIONS

◆ **Make the Leather Spacers:**

1. Using the pattern as a guide, cut two buck skin rectangles, each ⅜" x 1½". Round the corners.
2. Punch six small holes in each according to the pattern.

◆ **Warp the Loom:**

See "Loom-Woven Beadwork" in the Beadwork Techniques chapter for more information.

1. Cut six 25" lengths of round leather lacing.
2. Tie the lacing pieces together at one end.
3. Thread one of the spacers on the pieces of leather lacing.
4. Secure the knotted end of the lacing at one end of the loom. Warp the loom with lacing every third row, making the spaces between the warp threads wide enough for 5mm shell tube beads.

Leather Spacer Patterns

Pattern for
5-hole
spacer
Cut 2 from
buck skin

Pattern for
single-hole
spacer
Cut 2 from
buck skin

5. Secure the lacing pieces tightly at the other end of the loom. Slide the buck skin spacer to the beginning end of loom.

◆ **Add the Beads:**

1. Thread a beading needle with 30" of beading thread. If you are right-handed, securely knot the thread on the top left leather lacing. If you are left-handed, knot the thread on the top right leather lacing.
2. Thread five shell tube beads on the needle and thread. Pass the thread with the beads under the warped loom. Press the beads up between each warp lacing.
3. Bring the needle above the warp lacing and pass the needle back through the beads over each warp lacing.
4. Loom weave beads to a length of 12". Allowing 2" for the clasp, this will make a choker 14" long. Add or delete rows of beads for your desired size.
5. When the weaving is the desired length, remove it from the loom. Thread the remaining leather spacer tightly against the last row of beads. Tie a knot in each lacing cord next to the leather spacer.
6. Using the pattern provided, cut two buck skin rectangles, each ⅜" x ½". Round the corners. Punch an ⅛" hole in the center of each rectangle.
7. Thread all six lacing cords at one end of the choker through the center hole of one leather spacer. Thread one side of the clasp on one lacing cord. Wrap sinew tightly around the leather lacing and clasp. Make several wraps. Knot sinew securely. Thread the sinew tail back through the wraps. Cut the tail.
8. Repeat step 7 on the other end of the choker to attach the other side of the clasp.
9. *Option:* Wrap the metal hook and eye with sinew. Knot the sinew and run the tail back through several wraps. Cut the tail. ❏

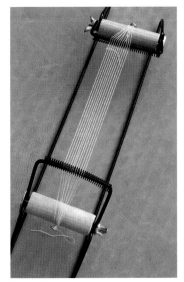

THUNDERBIRD BRACELET

Thunderbirds were giant birds of legend — possibly condors or turkey buzzards or large eagles — that were believed to create thunder and lightning as they flew through the sky. Thunderbirds symbolize power, but interpretations vary from tribe to tribe. Indians in the Pacific Northwest used thunderbirds on their totems and canoes, believing the thunderbird image protected them from harm, while the Plains Indians feared the thunderbird, believing it would come and raid their villages, carrying off small children.

This bracelet features three thunderbirds arranged in a row. It is 1" wide and 7¼" long.

SUPPLIES

◆ Seed beads, size 11/0 – Turquoise, black, red, orange, yellow, green, dark turquoise

◆ Deer skin

◆ 2 snaps, 3/16"

◆ Beading thread

◆ Beading needle

◆ Tracing paper

◆ Transfer paper and stylus

Optional: Beading loom

INSTRUCTIONS

1. Trace the pattern outline and transfer to the deer skin.
2. Using the lane stitch and following the design on the Beading Chart, sew the beads on the leather. Run the needle through the inside of the leather strip to hide the threads. (Fig. 1) *See also "Lane Stitch" section in the Beadwork Techniques chapter.*
3. Bead the two long sides and one end with seed beads, using the fret edging technique. *See the "Fret Edging" section in the Beadwork Techniques chapter for more information.*
4. Sew the snap parts at each end of the bracelet, placing the end with the fret edge on top.

Option: The bead work could, instead, be loomed, then glued on leather strip. If using a loom, thread it with 11 warp threads. ❑

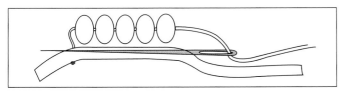

Photo 1 – Back of bracelet

Fig. 1 – Lane Stitch

Beading Chart

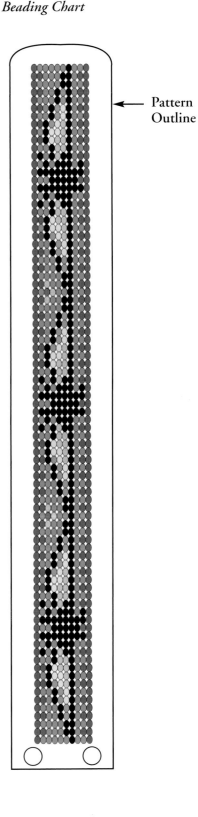

Pattern Outline

MEDICINE NECKLACE

The Hupa Indian Tribe originally lived in the river valleys near the Pacific Ocean in Northern California. They were hunters and fishers who lived in cedar plank houses and were known for their fine pipes (made by men) and baskets (made by women). This leather pouch is inspired by the ones worn by Hupas to carry small articles, which were decorated with shells and animal teeth. Because of their proximity to the sea, they used lots of seashells in their ornamentation.

The finished length is 25".

SUPPLIES

◆ Elk skin

◆ 8 cowrie shells, 12mm x 18mm

◆ 38 spiral shells, 5mm x 8mm

◆ 15 mother of pearl nuggets

◆ Artificial sinew

◆ Beading thread

◆ Beading needle

◆ Glover's leather needle

◆ Tracing paper

◆ Transfer paper and stylus

INSTRUCTIONS

◆ **Cut & Sew:**

1. Trace the patterns provided. Transfer to the elk skin. Cut out.
2. With smooth sides facing out, place the front panel on the pouch back. Whip stitch around the sides and bottom, using a glover's needle and sinew.
3. Whip stitch around the edge of the flap.

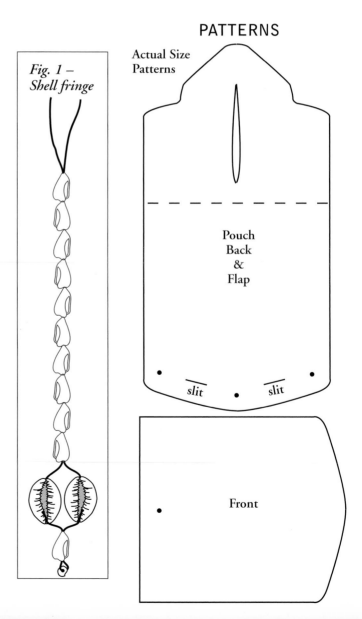

Fig. 1 –
Shell fringe

PATTERNS

Actual Size
Patterns

Pouch
Back
&
Flap

slit   *slit*

Front

◆ Make the Shell Fringe:

The placement of the shell fringe is marked by dots on the pattern.

1. Secure beading thread at the center bottom of the pouch. Thread 10 spiral shells on the thread. Add a cowrie shell, a spiral shell, and a mother of pearl nugget. Bring the needle around the nugget, then back through the spiral shell. Add a second cowrie shell then go back through ten spiral shells. Secure beading thread on pouch. See Fig. 1.

2. Add two more lengths shell fringe, one on each side.

◆ Make the Shell Closure:

1. Cut a slit on the flap as shown on the pattern.

2. At the dot marked on the pouch front pattern, secure beading thread. Thread three spiral shells, a cowrie shell, two spiral shells, and a mother of pearl nugget on the thread. Bring the needle around the nugget, then back through the two spiral shells. Add a second cowrie shell then go back through three spiral shells. Secure beading thread on pouch.

◆ Make the Leather Fringe:

1. Cut two 12" elk skin strips ⅛" wide.

2. Cut two slits in the bottom of the pouch as marked on the pattern.

3. Thread a leather strip through each slit. Center and tie the strip to make fringe.

4. Sew a mother of pearl nugget on each of the four ends. ❏

◆ Make the Strap:

1. Cut three 36" strips of elk skin ⅛" wide. Tightly wrap and knot sinew around all three strips 4" from one end. Braid strips to 4" from other end. Wrap and knot with sinew.

2. Sew one end of the braid to each side of the top of the pouch, letting the loose ends hang free.

3. Sew a mother of pearl nugget at the end of each 4" fringe, using beading needle and thread.

TURTLE FETISH NECKLACE & EARRINGS

The turtle is a symbol of Mother Earth. He represents patience, self-reliance, tenacity, and longevity. He is also associated with non-violent defense and with being a skillful navigator through life's obstacles. This necklace was inspired by a Zuni Pueblo design. Today, the Zuni Pueblo is nestled in a beautiful valley surrounded by mesas about 150 miles west of Albuquerque, NM. The Pueblo encompasses approximately 450,000 acres.

The finished length of the necklace is 28".

SUPPLIES

- 80 bamboo coral nuggets, 10-15mm
- 7 black carved horn turtle fetishes
- 10 turquoise nuggets, 12mm x 15mm
- 2.4mm sterling silver plated beads
- Turquoise nuggets, 4-6mm
- Silver toggle clasp
- Silver crimp beads
- 2 silver-plated round beads, 6mm
- 2 silver fish hook ear wires
- Bead stringing wire, .015"
- Needlenose pliers

INSTRUCTIONS

Necklace:

1. Cut a 40" length of bead stringing wire. Thread a crimp bead on the wire. Thread the end of the wire through one side of the clasp, then back through the crimp bead, leaving a 1½" tail. Crimp the bead next to clasp.
2. Thread a 2.4 mm silver bead and 2" of turquoise nuggets on the wire and over the wire tail.
3. Thread a 2.4mm silver bead, three coral nuggets, a silver bead, a turquoise nugget, a silver bead, and three coral nuggets on the wire.
4. Repeat this sequence three times: Add a 2.4mm silver bead, five coral nuggets, a silver bead, a turtle, a silver bead, and five coral nuggets.
5. Add a silver bead, five coral nuggets, a turquoise nugget, a silver bead, five coral nuggets, a silver bead and the center turtle.
6. Reverse the sequence in steps 3, 4, and 5 and repeat to make the other side of the necklace.
7. Thread a crimp bead on the end of the wire. Thread the wire through the other side of the clasp, then back through the crimp bead and several turquoise nuggets. Pull the wires taut. Crimp the bead. Cut the wire tail.

Earrings:

1. Cut a 12" length of bead stringing wire. Thread a turtle fetish on the wire and center it on the wire.
2. On each side of the turtle, add a 2.4mm silver bead and 1" of turquoise nuggets. Bring the wire ends together.
3. Thread both wires through a 2.4mm silver bead, a 6mm silver bead, a crimp bead, and an ear wire. Bring both wire ends around the ear wire loop, then back through the crimp bead and 6mm bead. Pull wires taut. Crimp bead. Cut wire tails.
4. Repeat steps 1 through 3 to make the other earring. ❏

109

ZIG-ZAG ANKLE BRACELET

Horn beads in two colors are combined to make an arrow design on an ankle bracelet that was made on a beading loom. Arrows are a symbol of the direction of travel.

The finished size is 1" x 9".

SUPPLIES

- ◆ Black horn rice beads, 4mm x 8mm
- ◆ Antiqued natural horn rice beads, 4mm x 8mm
- ◆ Hook and eye clasp, size 1
- ◆ Beading thread
- ◆ Beading needle
- ◆ Fray preventive liquid
- ◆ Beading loom

INSTRUCTIONS

◆ Warp the Loom:

1. Cut four 30" lengths of beading thread. Tie the ends together at one end.
2. Warp the loom with a thread in every fourth row, making warp threads wide enough for the 8mm bone beads.
3. Secure the threads tightly at other end of loom.

◆ Make the Bead Weaving:

See "Loom-Woven Beadwork" for detailed instructions.

1. Thread a beading needle with 30" of beading thread. If you're right-handed, securely knot the thread on the top left leather lacing. If you are left handed, knot thread on the top right leather lacing.
2. Thread three horn beads on the needle and thread in the colors specified in the Beading Chart. Pass the thread and beads under the warped loom. Press beads up between each warp thread.
3. Bring the needle above the warp threads and pass the needle back through beads over each warp thread.
4. Continue, following the sequence in the Beading Chart, to loom weave beads to 9" or your desired length.

◆ Finish:

1. Remove the weaving from the loom. Knot two outer warp threads at one end together securely. Knot the other two warp threads. (Fig. 1)

Fig. 1 – Tying off the warp threads.

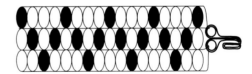

2. Tie the hook on one end with the warp threads. Knot securely. Dot knots with fray preventive. Weave the thread tails back through several rows of beads. (Fig. 2)
3. Repeat step 2 to attach the eye at the other end. Knot tails and trim. ❏

Fig. 2 – Attaching the hook with the warp threads.

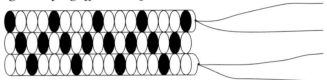

Beading Chart

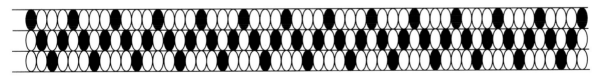

PEYOTE STITCH ARROWHEAD AMULET

Two powerful Native American symbols are combined here: The arrow, symbolizing force, direction, and power, and the feather, symbolizing prayers and ideas. The peyote stitch, also known as the gourd stitch, is an off-loom beading technique. There are a number of variations of this stitch.

SUPPLIES

◆ Arrowhead
◆ Seed beads, size 11/0 – Black, dark red
◆ 2 silver feather charms, 24mm
◆ Silver ring, 10mm
◆ Silver lanyard hook, 23mm
◆ Beading thread
◆ Beading needle

INSTRUCTIONS

◆ Bead the Arrowhead Neck:

1. Round one – See Fig. 1. Thread a beading needle with 30" of beading thread. String red seed beads around the neck (the narrow part) of the arrowhead. Tie thread in a circle, leaving a 3" thread tail on the back of the arrowhead.
2. Round two – See Fig. 2. Pass the needle through the first bead left of the knot. Pick up a black bead, skip a bead and go through the next bead. Repeat around the arrowhead neck until you're back to the starting point.
3. Round three – Go through the first beads on row 2 as shown in Fig. 3. Pick up a red bead and go through a black bead in row two. Continue around the arrowhead neck.
4. Round four – See Fig. 4. Go through the first bead on round three. Pick up a red bead and go through a red bead in row three. Continue around the arrowhead neck. Run the needle and thread back through several beads until you get to the thread tail. Knot the threads.

◆ Bead the Hanging Loop:

See Figs. 1 through 4.

1. Round one – Pass the needle through the beads on the arrowhead neck, bringing the thread out at the side of the arrowhead. Thread 80 red beads on the thread. Pass the needle through a bead on other side of arrowhead neck to complete round one of loop. (Fig. 1)
2. Round two – See round two in Fig. 2 to complete the second row of the loop with black beads.
3. Round three – See round three in Fig. 3 to complete the third row of the loop with red beads.
4. Round four – See round four in Fig. 4 to complete the fourth row of the loop with red beads. Knot the thread on the side of the arrowhead. Run the tail back through several beads. Trim the tail.

◆ Add the Feather Fringe:

1. Thread a beading needle with 20" of beading thread.
2. Fringe 1 – Pass the needle through a seed bead on the back of the arrowhead neck. Thread five red seed beads and a black seed bead on the needle and thread. Repeat the sequence four more times. Loop the needle and thread around the top loop of one of the feather charms, then pass it back through the seed beads in the fringe. Pull the thread so the beads hang loosely and allow the fringe to dangle. Knot the thread to the tail thread.
3. Fringe 2 – Pass the needle through another seed bead on the back of the arrowhead neck. Thread three red seed beads and a black seed bead on the needle and thread. Thread five red seed beads and a black seed bead on the needle and thread. Repeat five more times. Loop the needle and thread around the top loop of the other feather charm, then back through the seed beads in the fringe. Pull the thread so the beads hang loosely and allow the fringe to dangle. Knot the thread to the tail thread.
4. Dot the knots with fray preventive. Thread the tails back through several beads. Trim the thread tails.

◆ Attach the Lanyard Hook:

1. Open the 10mm jump ring. Install on the hanging loop.
2. Put the lanyard hook on the jump ring. ❏

Fig. 1

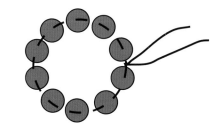

Fig. 2

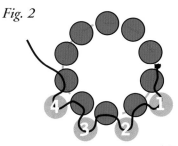

Fig. 3

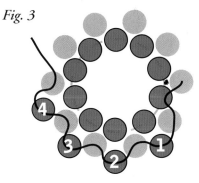

Fig. 4

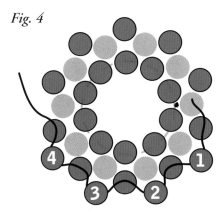

OMAHA STYLE BELT BAG

The Omaha Indians are from Nebraska, and the design for the beading on this bag was inspired by an Omaha shirt design. Metal jinglers were constructed from scraps of copper, brass or tobacco tins. Jinglers were used to decorate pouches, clothing, knifesheaths and moccasins.

The lane stitch, used to sew the beads to the leather, is an off-loom beading technique that is useful for making geometric designs. This bag is 4½" wide and 18" long, including the fringe.

SUPPLIES

- ◆ Elk skin
- ◆ Opaque seed beads, size 11/0 – White, turquoise, dark red, yellow, black
- ◆ Opaque black seed beads, size 10/0 (for the fret edging)
- ◆ 13 black beads, 5mm
- ◆ 13 brass beads, 8mm
- ◆ 13 brass beads, 5mm
- ◆ 13 beads, 3mm (These go inside the cones.)
- ◆ 35 brass cones, ¾"
- ◆ Beading needle
- ◆ Beading thread
- ◆ Artificial sinew
- ◆ Leather glover's needle
- ◆ Yard stick
- ◆ Marker
- ◆ Craft knife

INSTRUCTIONS

◆ **Cut & Assemble:**

See patterns on page 116.

1. Using the pattern diagram provided, draw the pattern on the elk skin. Cut out.
2. Place the inside front piece on top of the pouch back piece with wrong sides together. Whip stitch the side seams, using a glover's needle with artificial sinew. Sew a running stitch along the bottom of the pouch above the fringe line.

◆ **Add the Bead Work:**

Complete the bead work before fringing the pouch. Follow the Beading Chart on page 116, working in vertical rows. See the "Lane Stitch" section in the Beadwork Techniques chapter.

1. Use the Lane Stitch technique to sew the beads to the right side of the flap, using a beading needle and beading thread: Bring the needle up through the right side of the leather. Thread five beads on the needle and slide the needle through the thickness of leather to conceal the thread. (Fig. 1)

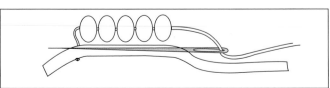

Fig. 1 – Lane Stitch

Continued on page 116

2. Bring the needle up through the leather. Add a second row of five seed beads below the first row. Continue, beading the vertical row of five beads according to pattern.

3. Move to the next row and complete a second vertical row of five beads, following the Beading Chart. When you finish beading all the rows, knot the thread. Pull the knot inside the leather.

4. Decorate the sides and bottom edge of the flap with 10/0 black seed beads, using the fret edging technique. *See Fig. 2 and the "Fret Edging" section in the Beadwork Techniques chapter for more information.*

◆ **Add the Cone Bead Fringe:**
See Fig. 3.

1. Starting at one corner of the bottom edge of the flap, run the beading needle and thread through a black bead on the fret edging as shown in Fig. 3. Add a 5mm black bead, an 8mm brass bead, a 5mm brass bead, a brass cone, and a 3mm bead.

2. Pass the needle back through the cone, the 5mm brass bead, the 8mm brass bead, and the 5mm black bead.

3. Pass the needle back through the same 10mm black seed bead. Pull the thread taut and knot the thread on the inside of the flap.

4. Skip four black beads on the fret edging. Bring the thread and needle through the next black bead over, and repeat steps 1 through 3 to add another set of beads with a cone.

5. Repeat the process to attach 13 cones along the bottom edge of the front flap.

◆ **Cut the Fringe:**

1. Cut 12" of elk skin below the pouch into fringe strips 3/16" wide.

2. Taper the ends of each fringe strip.

3. Thread each tapered fringe end through the hole in the small end of a brass cone. Pull the fringe strip through the cone and knot ¾" from the end. Pull the knot inside the cone. Cut off the fringe tail below the bottom of the cone.

◆ **Cut the Slits:**

Cut six 1½" slits across the top part of the pouch back, as shown in the pattern diagram.

To wear: Thread a belt through the slits. ❏

Beading Chart (Actual size)

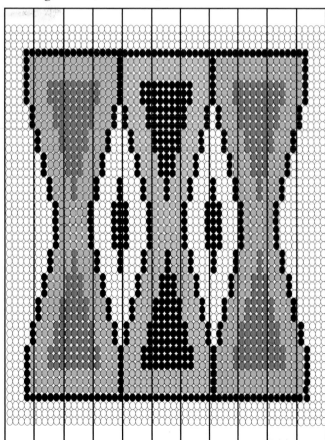

Fig. 2 – Fret Edging

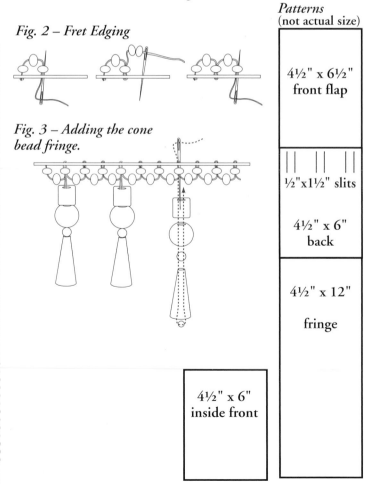

Fig. 3 – Adding the cone bead fringe.

Patterns
(not actual size)

4½" x 6½"
front flap

½"x1½" slits

4½" x 6"
back

4½" x 12"
fringe

4½" x 6"
inside front

LIQUID SILVER NECKLACE SET

Silver beads and coins were brought to the Indians of the Southwest by Spanish traders. Turquoise is a gemstone native to the Southwest region.

The finished length of this necklace is 18".

SUPPLIES

- 238 pieces liquid silver
- 2 sterling silver cone bead caps
- 19 silver plated beads, 2.4mm
- 4 silver 3-hole spacer bars, 14mm
- Turquoise seed beads, size 11/0
- 2 turquoise round beads, 6mm
- Silver clasp
- 2 silver eye pins
- 2 silver jump rings
- 2 silver fish hook ear wires
- 16 silver seed beads
- Beading thread
- Beading needle
- Fray preventive liquid
- Needlenose pliers
- Roundnose pliers
- Scissors

INSTRUCTIONS

◆ **Make the Necklace:**

1. Cut three 30" lengths of beading thread and knot on an eye pin. Dot each knot with fray preventive liquid. Tie another knot in each thread, then clip the thread tails.
2. Thread the eye pin through a cone bead cap. (Fig. 1)
3. Trim the end of the eye pin ⅜" from the end of the cone. Form a loop in eye pin with roundnose pliers. (Fig. 2)
4. Join the eye pin to one side of the clasp with a jump ring. (Fig. 3)
5. Thread all three threads through a 6mm turquoise bead. Separate the threads.
6. On each thread, add seven liquid silver pieces, seven turquoise seed beads, a 2.4mm silver round bead, seven turquoise seed beads, seven liquid silver pieces, and a three hole spacer bar. Repeat the beads in this sequence four times, leaving off the spacer bar at the end of the fourth repetition.
7. Bring all thread ends together. Thread all thread ends through a 6mm turquoise round bead. Knot thread ends on an eye pin. Dot knots with glue. Knot again and cut thread tails. Thread eye pin through cone bead cap. Trim eye pin end ⅜" from cone end. Form a loop in eye pin with round nose pliers. Join eye pin to clasp with a jump ring.

◆ **Make the Earrings:**

1. Cut a 14" length of beading thread. Thread a 2.4mm silver round bead, seven liquid silver pieces, seven turquoise seed beads, a 2.4mm silver round bead, seven turquoise seed beads, and seven liquid silver pieces. Bring the thread ends together. Knot the thread.
2. Place eight silver seed beads on one thread above the knot. Pass the remaining thread through all eight silver seed beads. Knot the thread ends together to make a hanging loop. Dot knots with glue. Pass the thread tails back through the bead loop. Trim the thread tails. Add a fish hook ear wire on the hanging loop.
3. Repeat the steps 1 and 2 to make the other earring. ❏

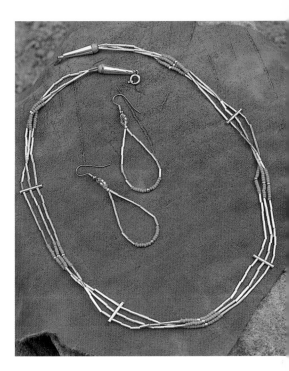

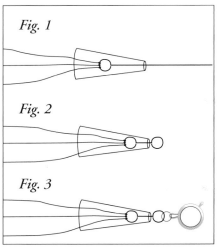

Fig. 1

Fig. 2

Fig. 3

BONE FEATHER NECKLACE & EARRINGS

Feathers are a common Native American symbol with many meanings – they are symbols of prayers, the source of ideas, and marks of honor. They are said to possess the attributes of the bird they came from (goose feathers for long flight, eagle feathers for honor and valor). These feathers are carved from bone. When arranged in a circle, feathers are related to the sun.

The finished length of this necklace is 16".

SUPPLIES

◆ Seed beads, size 10/0 – Turquoise, silver

◆ 15 carved bone feather pendants, 11mm x 27mm

◆ 47 round bone beads, 5mm

◆ Silver clasp

◆ Crimp bead

◆ 2 silver fish hook ear wires

◆ Beading needle

◆ Beading thread

◆ Scissors

◆ Fray preventive liquid

◆ Needlenose pliers

INSTRUCTIONS

◆ **Make the Necklace:**

1. Thread beading needle with 35" to 40" of beading thread. Tie one end to one side of the clasp in a square knot, leaving a 4" tail. See Fig. 1. (This tail will be threaded through several beads of finished necklace.) Secure the thread around the clasp a second time. Knot the thread. Dot the knot with fray preventive liquid.

2. Thread seed beads and round bone beads as shown in Fig. 2.

3. For the feather drop, thread three turquoise seeds, a 5mm bone, 3 turquoise seeds, a silver seed, a turquoise seed, a feather pendant, a turquoise seed, a silver seed, and 3 turquoise seeds. Pass the needle back through the 5mm bone and 3 turquoise seed beads.

4. Continue beading necklace to the next drop, as shown in Fig. 3. Continue the same beading sequence until you have added 13 feather pendant drops.

5. Finish beading the necklace according to Fig. 4. Add a crimp bead and the other side of the clasp on the thread. Pass the needle back through the crimp bead and several beads. Pull the thread taut. Crimp bead.

◆ **Make the Earrings:**

See Fig. 5.

1. Thread a beading needle with 25" of thread. Thread 8 turquoise seed beads on the thread. Form a loop and knot the thread, leaving a 4" tail. Pass the needle back through the beads to secure the hanging loop.

2. Thread beads as shown. Form the bottom loop with 3 turquoise seeds, 1 silver seed, 1 turquoise seed, a bone feather, 1 turquoise seed, 1 silver seed, and 3 turquoise

seeds. Pass the thread back through the row of beads to the knot. Knot the threads. Dot knot with fray preventive. Run the thread tails back through several beads. Trim the ends of the thread tails.

3. Add a fish hook ear wire to the beaded hanging loop.

4. Repeat steps 1 through 3 to make the other earring. ❏

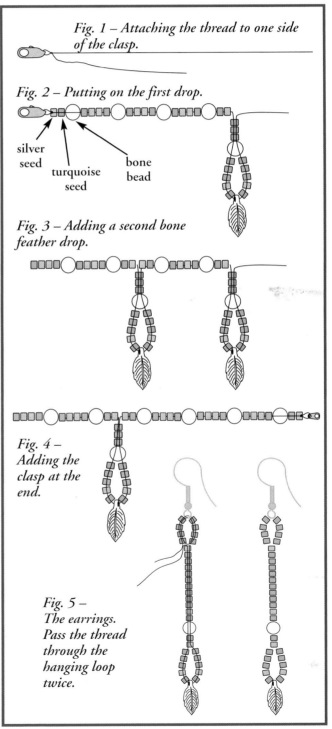

Fig. 1 – Attaching the thread to one side of the clasp.

Fig. 2 – Putting on the first drop.

silver seed

turquoise seed

bone bead

Fig. 3 – Adding a second bone feather drop.

Fig. 4 – Adding the clasp at the end.

Fig. 5 – The earrings. Pass the thread through the hanging loop twice.

HORN SPIDER NECKLACE SET

The spider was an important symbol to the Mississippian culture and is especially associated with women. It symbolizes weaving, fertility, the center of the earth, and balance, and harmony. This necklace of black horn beads recalls a spider's web.

The finished length of the necklace is 16".

SUPPLIES

- beads, size 11/0 – Yellow matte, deep red, gunmetal silver
- Black horn rice beads, 4mm x 8mm
- 4 round gold bone beads
- Gold clasp
- 2 gold fish hook ear wires
- Beading needle
- Beading thread
- Fray preventive liquid
- Scissors

INSTRUCTIONS

◆ **Make the Necklace:**

1. Thread a beading needle with 40" of beading thread. Tie one end to one side of the clasp in a square knot, leaving a 4" tail. (The tail will be threaded back through several beads of the finished necklace.) Secure the thread around the clasp a second time. Knot again. Dot the knot with fray preventive. (Fig. 1)

2. Thread beads in this order, as shown in Fig. 2: a gunmetal seed bead, a black horn (#1), a gunmetal seed, a red seed, 3 yellow seeds, a red seed.

3. Repeat the sequence with a second set of beads. (Fig. 2)

4. Add a gunmetal seed, a black horn (#3), a gunmetal seed, a red seed, a 4mm gold horn, a gunmetal seed, a black horn (#4), and a gunmetal seed. (Fig. 2)

6. Add this seed bead sequence: a red, 3 yellow, a red, a gunmetal, a red, 3 yellow, a red. (Fig. 3)

7. Add a gunmetal seed, a black horn (#5), and a gunmetal seed. Repeat the seed bead sequence in step 6.

8. Add a gunmetal seed, a black horn (#6), a gunmetal seed, a red seed, 3 yellow seeds, a red seed, a 4mm gold horn, a red seed, 3 yellow seeds, and a red seed. Pass the needle back through the black horn bead (#6) and both gunmetal seed beads.

9. Add the seed bead sequence in step 6, a gunmetal seed, a black horn (#7), and a gunmetal seed. Repeat the seed bead sequence in step 6.

Continued on page 122

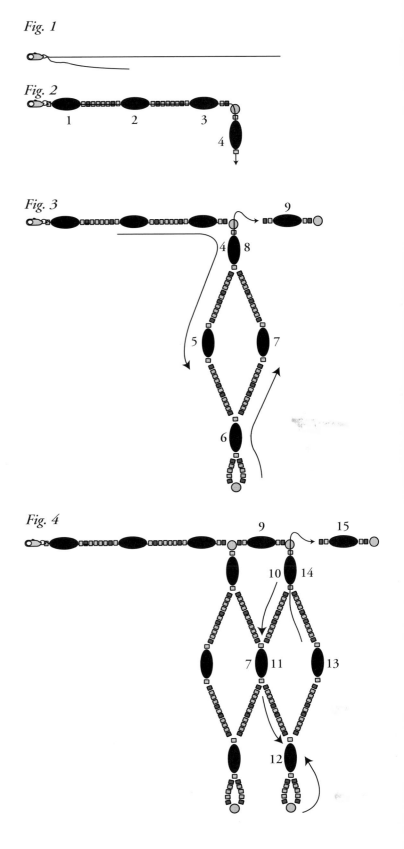

Fig. 1

Fig. 2

Fig. 3

Fig. 4

10. Pass the needle back through the black horn bead (#4, #8) and both gunmetal seeds. Pass needle back through the 4mm gold horn. Add a red seed, a gunmetal seed, a black horn (#9), a gunmetal seed, a red seed, and a 4mm gold horn. This completes the first drop. (Fig. 3)

11. Start the second drop (Fig. 4), passing the thread through black horn bead #7 to connect the drops. Continue adding and connecting drops, making 17 in all as shown in photo. As new lengths of thread are needed, knot the tail of the new thread securely to the old thread tail in a square knot. Dot the knot with fray preventive and continue beading over the knot and thread tails.

12. While you have completed the final drop, finish necklace with the reverse of the sequence pictured in Fig. 2.

13. Tie the thread to the remaining side of the clasp in a square knot. Dot knot with fray preventive liquid. Pass the thread tail back through several beads and trim the end.

14. Thread the beginning tail back through several beads. Trim the end.

◆ **Make the Earrings:**

See Fig. 5.

1. Thread a beading needle with 25" of thread. Thread on 8 yellow seed beads. Form a hanging loop and knot the thread, leaving a 4" tail. Pass the needle back through the beads to secure the hanging loop.

2. Thread earring beads as shown. Form the bottom loop and pass the thread back through the row of beads to the knot. Knot the threads. Dot knot with fray preventive liquid. Run thread tails back through several beads. Trim the ends.

3. Add a fish hook ear wire to the beaded hanging loop.

4. Repeat steps 1 through 3 to make the other earring. ❏

Fig. 5

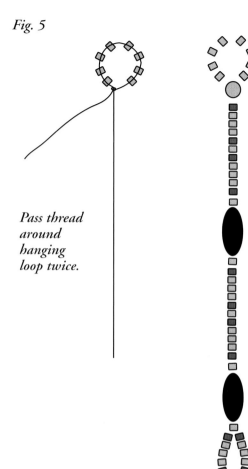

Pass thread around hanging loop twice.

BUTTERFLY BARRETTE

There are numerous butterfly legends in Native American lore. According to a Papago story, the Creator gathered the beautiful things of the earth — a spot of sunlight, a handful of blue sky, the white from cornmeal, the shadow of playing children, the black of a girl's hair, yellow from falling leaves, green from pine needles, the red, purple and orange colors of the flowers — and put them in a bag, which he presented to a group of playing children as a gift. When the children opened the bag, hundreds of colorful butterflies flew out.

The finished size is 3½" x 2½".

SUPPLIES

◆ Black leather

◆ Seed beads, size 11/0 – Silver, red, green, dark turquoise, opaque black, turquoise, pink, orange

◆ Beading thread

◆ Beading needle

◆ Cardboard

◆ French-style barrette back, 58mm

INSTRUCTIONS

1. Using the Beading Chart as a guide, sew beads to create the butterfly design on the smooth side of a piece of black leather, using the Lane Stitch technique. *See the "Lane Stitch" section in the Beadwork Techniques section for more information.*

2. Trim the leather so it is ½" larger all around than the beading.

3. Cut a second piece of leather the same size as the first piece.

4. Cut two pieces of cardboard, each measuring 3⅛" W x 2¼" D. Slightly round the corners.

5. Sew a running stitch around the beaded piece of leather ⅛" from the edges. Center one piece of cardboard on the suede side of the leather. Pull the thread to gather the stitches tightly around the cardboard. Knot the thread. Repeat on the other piece of leather and the remaining piece of cardboard.

6. Place the two leather pieces back to back, with the smooth sides of the leather out and the cardboard sides touching. Join the two pieces by stitching a fret edge around all the sides with black seed beads. *See the "Fret Edging" section in the Beadwork Techniques chapter for more information.*

7. Sew the barrette back on the back (unbeaded) side of the leather, using black thread.

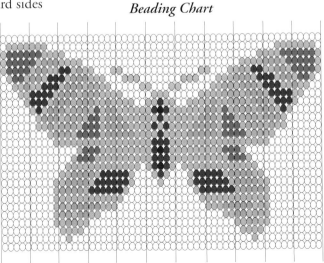

Beading Chart

HEISHI NECKLACE & EARRINGS

Heishi comes from the Santo Domingo word for shell. This necklace, made from shell heishi beads in two colors, was inspired by the Monache and other tribes of Southern California where shells were used for decoration.

The finished length of the necklace is 24".

SUPPLIES

- ◆ White clamshell heishi, 4-5mm
- ◆ Dark penshell heishi, 4-5mm
- ◆ 8 white bone beads, 4mm
- ◆ Silver hook and eye clasp
- ◆ 2 cone bead caps, 15mm
- ◆ 2 fish hook ear wires
- ◆ Silver crimp beads
- ◆ Bead stringing wire, .015
- ◆ Needlenose pliers

INSTRUCTIONS

◆ **Make the Necklace:**

1. Cut three 40" lengths of bead stringing wire. Thread one end of all three wires through a cone bead cap, a crimp bead and one side of the clasp. Loop the wires through the clasp, then back through the crimp bead and cone bead cap, leaving 2" wire tails. Pull wires taut. Crimp bead.

2. Thread three bone beads on all the wires, next to the cone bead cap. (Fig. 1)

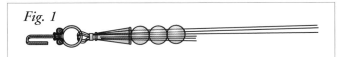

Fig. 1

3. Separate the wires.

4. Bead the outer strand. On one wire, add 8" of white heishi. (The total white length is 8½", including the three white bone beads). Next add 1½" of brown heishi, 2" of white heishi, 2½" of brown heishi, and 3" of white heishi. To complete the strand, reverse the order, starting with 2½" of brown heishi. (Fig. 2)

5. Bead the middle strand. On one wire, add one white bone bead and 10½" of white heishi. (The total white length is 10½", including the one white bone bead). Next, add 1½" of brown heishi and 5" of white heishi. To complete the middle

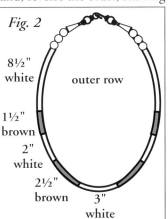

Fig. 2

8½" white — outer row

1½" brown

2" white

2½" brown   3" white

strand, reverse the order, starting with 1½" of brown heishi. (Fig. 3)

6. Bead the inner strand. On the remaining wire, add one white bone bead and 7½" of white heishi. (The total white length is 7½", including the one white bone bead). Next add 1½" of brown heishi and 8" of white heishi. To complete the inner strand, reverse the order, starting with 1½" of brown heishi. (Fig. 4)

7. Thread the wire ends of the middle strand and inner strand through the three white bone beads on the outer strand.

8. Bring all the wire ends together and thread through a cone bead cap, a crimp bead, and the remaining side of the clasp on all three wires. Loop the wires through the clasp, then back through the crimp bead and cone bead cap. Pull threads taut. Crimp bead. Cut the wire tails.

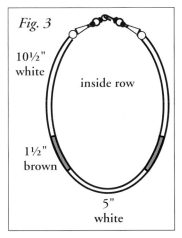

Fig. 3

10½" white

inside row

1½" brown

5" white

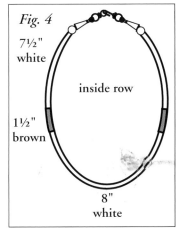

Fig. 4

7½" white

inside row

1½" brown

8" white

◆ **Make the Earrings:**

1. Cut 12" of bead stringing wire. Thread 1½" of white heishi, 1" of brown heishi, 1½" of white heishi, and a crimp bead on the wire. Thread both wire ends through crimp bead and several heishi, forming a circle. (Fig. 5) Pull wires taut. Crimp bead. Cut wire tails.

2. Add a fish hook ear wire around the crimp bead.

3. Repeat steps 1 and 2 to make the other earring. ❏

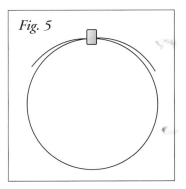

Fig. 5

GEMS OF THE SOUTHWEST NECKLACE & EARRINGS

The gemstones in this necklace – agate, coral, turquoise, malachite, hematite, and lapis – were used by many Southwestern tribes, including Navajo, Hopi, Zuni, Apache, Pecos, Ealapai, and Mojave. Shell beads and obsidian came from trade with neighboring tribes in California.

Use the photo as a guide for how to arrange the colors and various shapes, or create your own arrangement.

The finished length of the necklace is 28".

SUPPLIES

- ◆ Buffalo head coin button
- ◆ Pewter round beads, 5mm
- ◆ Crazy lace (ochre) agate round beads, 5mm
- ◆ Red bamboo coral nuggets
- ◆ Obsidian rondelles, 5mm
- ◆ Turquoise nuggets, 10mm
- ◆ Lapis round beads, 8mm
- ◆ Lapis nuggets, 8mm
- ◆ Turquoise round beads, 6mm and 8mm
- ◆ Hematite round beads, 4mm and 6mm
- ◆ Onyx round beads, 3mm, 6mm, and 8mm
- ◆ Jasper, malachite, quartz, turquoise nuggets
- ◆ Red matte e beads
- ◆ Pewter spacer assortment
- ◆ Pewter bead cap assortment
- ◆ Crimp beads
- ◆ Bead stringing wire, .015
- ◆ 2 ear wires
- ◆ Needlenose pliers

INSTRUCTIONS

◆ Make the Necklace:

1. Cut two 40" lengths of bead stringing wire. Thread a crimp bead and twelve 5mm pewter beads on one end of both wires. (Fig. 1)
2. Form the beads on the wire into a loop and thread the ends of the two wires back through the crimp bead, leaving 2" tails. Pull wires taut. Crimp bead. (Fig. 2)
3. Thread 4" of beads, nuggets, and spacers on both wires, placing a bamboo coral bead on the wires every 1½". Separate the two wires at 4". (Fig. 3)

4. On the outer strand, thread 23" of bead with a bamboo coral bead every 1½".
5. On the inner strand, thread 20" of beads, also placing a bamboo coral bead every 1½".
6. Bring the ends of both wires back together. Thread 4" of beads on both wires. Add a crimp bead.
7. Bring the ends of both wires through the shank of the buffalo button, then back through the crimp bead and several beads. Pull wires taut. Crimp bead.

◆ Make the Earrings:

1. Cut a 12" length of bead stringing wire. Thread 2¼" of beads and nuggets on the wire. Add a red bamboo coral nugget. Thread another 2¼" beads and nuggets on the wire. Bring the wire ends together.
2. Thread a 5mm hematite round bead and a crimp bead on both wires. Separate the wires.
3. Thread eight turquoise seed beads on one wire. Thread the second wire through the seed beads. Thread both wire ends through a crimp bead and several beads. Pull wires taut to make a bead loop. Crimp bead. Cut wire tails.
4. Attach the earring to a hook.
5. Repeat steps 1 through 4 to make the other earring. ❑

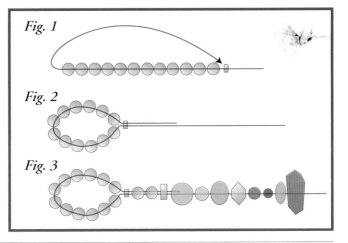

Fig. 1

Fig. 2

Fig. 3

Metric Conversion Chart

Inches to Millimeters and Centimeters

Inches	MM	CM	Inches	MM	CM
1/8	3	.3	2	51	5.1
1/4	6	.6	3	76	7.6
3/8	10	1.0	4	102	10.2
1/2	13	1.3	5	127	12.7
5/8	16	1.6	6	152	15.2
3/4	19	1.9	7	178	17.8
7/8	22	2.2	8	203	20.3
1	25	2.5	9	229	22.9
1-1/4	32	3.2	10	254	25.4
1-1/2	38	3.8	11	279	27.9
1-3/4	44	4.4	12	305	30.5

Yards to Meters

Yards	Meters	Yards	Meters
1/8	.11	3	2.74
1/4	.23	4	3.66
3/8	.34	5	4.57
1/2	.46	6	5.49
5/8	.57	7	6.40
3/4	.69	8	7.32
7/8	.80	9	8.23
1	.91	10	9.14
2	1.83		

Index